MW00333728

The *[New]* New Patriotism

JENNIFER BLACKBURN

© 2020 Jennifer Blackburn

ISBN 978-1-09833-424-6

All rights reserved. No part of this book may be reproduced or transmitted in
any form or by any means, electronic or mechanical, including photocopying,
recording, or by any information storage and retrieval system without the written
permission of the author, except where permitted by law.

For Catie, Tyler, Christine, Collin, Michael, and Bryce—
The future is yours to shape

Contents

INTRODUCTION

The idea and the passion for writing this book came, as we are re-experiencing scenes from our country's past, without a clear purpose on how we move forward as a nation. There is a growing enthusiasm for dramatic expression of our nation's problems without a real process for the solution. The peaceful protests designed to give voice to the unheard, are unfortunately overshadowed by the senseless and violent riots burning through American cities. I am not opposed to protest that has purpose and reason and is nonviolent; however, it is alarming to watch the number of Americans who did not cast a vote, but who are protesting violently. A significant number of these protestors, when asked, cannot articulate what they stand for, or for what they are opposed to. There is a clear disengagement in understanding our American history—the good and the bad—that has allowed us to arrive at the present moment.

Special interest groups looking for lemmings to represent their agenda manipulate youth, angst, and inexperience. These groups try to achieve strength in numbers to spread oppression of freedoms, develop a hate mentality, create chaos, engage the media, and promote violence. Human beings driven by anger and hate—rather than rational thought—dissolve into adopted behaviors with destructive consequences. There is a swell of hate and reactive behavior in our public spaces that has morphed through a generation raised on reality TV and immediate social media responders. This radical behavior bent on molding the minds of our youth bears a faint resemblance to the practice of foreign radicals in the Middle East and Africa.

We are experiencing racial tension and violence in our inner cities— an ebb and flow that repeats for over a century and a half. The conversation during these violent and often tragic circumstances revolves around narratives that center on victimization rather than a scaled opportunity to right wrongs through bottom-up change. Our society perches on a dangerous precipice. We are in desperate need of a redirect in how we articulate and create thinkers and doers in our country who value law and order, inclusiveness, raising our youth to higher standards, and working together peacefully to improve our society.

We need to change our culture of inequity. American democracy has not remained true to our founding principles. A lack of understanding and processing our history has led to a general population not inspired to embrace patriotism in America today. The truth is we do not mirror those principles in society. If we truly desire a democracy, we need to have difficult conversations, honest debates, and civil dialogue. All aspects of life require compromise. Our lawmakers are more engaged in creating sound bites, divisiveness, and hatred than connecting with a constituency. How do we collectively progress as a community, a city, a state, or a country? Rather than uplifting dialogue, negative banter has unfortunately become the order of the day. Great orators who remind us of our nation's historical significance, not just for the U.S. but also for the rest of the civilized world, are missing from the headlines and video stream.

There are two lessons from my high school history teacher, Mrs. Cannon, which I have found to ring true over the 35 years since I sat in her classroom: "History repeats itself," and "change is constant." I find myself thinking about these lessons more as I journey through life. We need to take more time trying to solve our issues, rather than casting blame. Consider how high the odds are that history will repeat itself if we continue to devolve into poisoned rhetoric rather than gaining perspective from the lessons of history. Technology has accelerated time to such a degree that objectivity becomes lost, and presentism takes over. The experiences of our triumphs and our failures in history fall prey to the lure of technology, progress, and efficiency. These historical lessons should not become obsolete.

Americans are in desperate need of a large-scale connection with the change-makers and orators of positive speak. We require the real change-makers to generate forward thinkers to benefit society's future, rather than their particular interests. How amazing would it be to connect with the concept that change has always been constant, to embrace the idea and harness the constancy of positive change to propel society forward?

I am not a politician, an economist, or a theologian. I am a 50-something, educated American woman who has been a single mom to two children, a blended family mom to six children, a wife, a designer, an artist, a volunteer, a business owner, a mid-level manager at a Fortune Eight company and an author. I am not affiliated or registered with a political party. I am a Patriot in the sense that I love the American Ideal—and we need to redefine what that represents in the 21st century. I am proud of my country and hope that we can begin redirecting our focus as an American society toward the core that made this country great. We need to recognize that the world is changing rapidly, but most importantly, <u>we</u> are the change agents.

CHAPTER 1

Patriotism versus Nationalism

It is not surprising that Americans have confused patriotism with nationalism. One of the main objectives in writing this book is to suggest that we change the conversation where patriotism is concerned—moving the country to more enlightened and emotionally intelligent patriotism. American patriotism incorporates freedoms, innovation, and a society that builds up its citizens and protects our way of life. Americans struggle to define a heritage that makes sense for the 21st century. Understanding our nationalistic history and how it is woven throughout American history can help understand American patriotism's journey. Our patriotic core is based on democracy and liberty. Nationalism becomes the driving force enlisted to protect democracy and freedom.

George Orwell describes his views on nationalism and patriotism in a 1945 article *Notes on Nationalism* in the British Magazine *Polemic*:

> *Nationalism is not to be confused with patriotism. Both words are normally used in so vague a way that any definition is liable to be challenged. Still, one must distinguish between them, since two different and even opposing ideas are*

involved. By 'patriotism' I mean devotion to a particular place and a specific way of life, which one believes to be the best in the world but has no wish to force other people. Patriotism is of its nature defensive, both militarily and culturally. Nationalism, on the other hand, is inseparable from the desire for power. The abiding purpose of every nationalist is to secure more power and prestige, not for himself but for the nation or other unit in which he has chosen to sink his individuality.

What drives conflict: The desire for power. What drives nationalism: The passion and self-determination to protect a nation's culture and freedoms no matter what a country has to do to achieve that goal. A patriot defends their country's culture and society. A patriot is not a provocateur. Politicians and political parties have differing views on how our culture and society should look. The word "patriotism" becomes a definition of convenience during election time. Its malleability is determined by the brand of patriotism benefiting a political party's agenda.

The word Nationalism has crept into the American lexicon over the years, most recently with *America First* becoming associated with nationalist thinking. Are we witnessing a new nationalism to regain a fading American patriotism? In the context of the role the U.S. has played across the globe as a moneylender, a brother in arms, and a peacekeeper—the America First ethos has been labeled nationalistic. As we drift toward putting our interests at home above protecting democracies abroad, does that resemble a provocateur, or does it resemble a nation preserving its heritage? American priorities placed first above global issues are not a simple task in the world of 21st-century global economies and geopolitics.

America First suggests that Americans are moving toward prioritizing a way of life that allows democracy to continue and flourish. We want to bring jobs and manufacturing back to the US, to encourage purchases in the US, rather than propping up our standard of living by purchasing cheaper goods made elsewhere. This mentality is not a desire for a power grab—it is a genuine redirect to shed consumer dependence and regain our independence. We are yearning for the American patriotic afterglow of the post-war years.

Change is constant, and history repeats itself. Change is why our two-party system has created an elected symmetry throughout our history. The majority selects the best option for what the majority sees as the country's most pressing needs at that time in history. We have elected 17 two-term U.S. presidents—with Lincoln, McKinley, and Nixon not serving their full second terms. Four out of five of our last sitting presidents have been two-term presidents. That had not happened since early in our history when Jefferson, Madison, and Monroe served two terms. It is interesting to reflect on our recent history in electing two-term presidents since the 1980s, a lifetime away for voters in their thirties and an entire voting career as someone in their fifties. What does this historical repeat of voting patterns suggest? Two-term presidencies usually indicate a society wanting stability amidst rapid change.

Our Founding Fathers Jefferson, Madison, and Monroe were the architects and signers of the framework for this country to function independently from England, to put the health and welfare of its citizenry first, and to end tyranny and oppression. Is that the beginning of patriotism or nationalism? Or both? Perhaps the idea that nationalism was the springboard for this country's birth, and that patriotism followed makes more sense. The "revolutionary" process to get early America from A to B—from tyranny to freedom—bears the markings of nationalism. It could be argued that patriotism was born as the American culture and way of life developed from our nationalism.

We revisit nationalism throughout our history, just as most countries do when their way of life is threatened or untenable. Revolution around the world to end tyranny defined a new way of life, born from nationalism. The advent of trade, a better quality of life, and the drive for personal independence brought a collective realization that people could change their society to a better place and system.

It began in 1776 with the American Revolution and then moved to the French Revolution in 1789, the Haitian Revolution in 1791, and the Irish Rebellion in 1798. Revolution triggered civil wars in the mid-1800s in Italy, the Germanic states, and Denmark. Revolution and nationalism swept through China and Russia, two massive countries whose 2,000-year-old histories were mostly sovereign and tyrannical. In early 1989, the Tiananmen Square Protests and the resulting massacre ultimately motivated the abandonment of Communism in parts of Asia and Africa. Later that same year, the hugely symbolic and triumphant fall of the Berlin Wall ended Communist life in East Germany. A successful domino effect wound its way through Poland, Hungary, Bulgaria, Czechoslovakia, and Romania. In 2010, beginning in Tunisia, anti-government protests and armed rebellions sparked the Arab Spring uprisings across North Africa and the Middle East against oppressive regimes. More recent history includes Brexit, the United Kingdom's withdrawal from the European Union, as another example of countries creating change to upend the status quo and regain their national identity or reject oppressive government practices.

Our American patriotism and the ability of any democracy to develop its heritage comes from citizen individuality. It comes from the rights of free countries to define their national pride through the individual contributions of free citizens. Most countries do not get to a place of developing patriotism without first going through a period of rebellion and then nationalism to protect and sustain their quality of life.

A dialogue involving nationalism often includes the subject of a strong military in the conversation. An enduring culture requires a strong, organized military that protects our borders and our way of life. It makes sense. Democratic nationalism does not intend to partition other countries. It exists to unite and strengthen our values and ideals rather than twisting them into the oppressive ideology we sought to change for the original 13 colonies.

Protecting the fabric of our American society is how we maintain a sense of order, pride, continued growth, success, and individual freedom. Those of us making careers outside of the military—entertainers, athletes, business people, teachers, higher education, the manufacturing industry, artists, etc. thrive because we have dedicated people to protect us. It is of great importance to remember that our soldiers and diplomats give the rest of us the freedom and the privilege to contribute and build an exceptional society.

A patriot's call to action: think about our founders' mindset when they created the framework for this amazing, first-of-its-kind nation. How can Americans preserve the Founders' carefully framed blueprint for a 21st-century American democracy?

CHAPTER 2

The American Patrimony

"Patrimony [**pa**-tru*h*-moh-nee] *A Latin rooted word that can mean an estate inherited from one's father or ancestors, or any quality, characteristic, etc., that is inherited—one's heritage"* —Merriam-Webster Dictionary.

There are certain iconic symbols and architecture of our American heritage or patrimony, such as the Declaration of Independence, the Bill of Rights, the Liberty Bell and the Stars and Stripes; monuments and buildings that include Independence Hall, the Lincoln Memorial, the Washington Monument and the Statue of Liberty. These are all symbols of the true essence of our American heritage. Our heritage—our national inheritance—is built on freedom and independence.

> *"We hold these Truths to be self-evident, that all men are created equal, that they are endowed by their Creator with certain unalienable Rights, that among these are Life, Liberty and the Pursuit of Happiness..."*— The Declaration of Independence

> *"Independence is my happiness, and I view things as they are, without regard to place or person; my country is the world,*

and my religion is to do good" — Thomas Paine, <u>Rights of Man</u>

...it's not a right-left issue. It's a right-wrong issue, and America has constantly been on the side of what's right. Because when it comes down to it, this is about keeping faith with the idea of America. Because America is an idea, isn't it?...That's how we see you around the world, as one of the greatest ideas in human history... the idea is that you and me are created equal ... that life is not meant to be endured, but enjoyed. The idea that if we have dignity, we have justice, then leave it to us—we'll do the rest. This country was the first to claw its way out of darkness and put that on paper. And God love you for it, because these aren't just American ideas anymore, there's no copyright on them. You brought them into the world, it's a wide world now, and I know Americans say they have a bit of the world in them, and you do. The family tree has lots of branches, but the thing is the world has a bit of America in it too. These truths... your truths ... they are self-evident in all of us. —Bono, Georgetown University, November 12, 2012

Freedoms—that is what our American core is all about. The right to vote, the right to choose, freedom of religion, speech, sexual orientation, and political persuasion are all freedoms to author our soul. With individual freedom, there should be shared dignity and respect for others. For one to be true, the other has to exist as well. If there is a dignity that human beings gain from independence and the courage of their convictions, then there should be respect for others' freedoms, independence, and personal beliefs. It is the Golden Rule many of us learned as children: "Do unto others as you would have them do unto you." One cannot insist on freedoms and independence without respecting others' differences-- in opinion, religion, and choice. All should be afforded those same freedoms, regardless of differing philosophies.

There are growing and disturbing movements in our country of groups interested in those freedoms as they apply to their agenda: groups who would like to hush those with differing opinions. This censorship of viewpoints has encouraged hate, irrational behavior, and intolerance of others who are different from ourselves. Patriotism in the United States has always been synonymous with freedom. We all need a straightforward reminder of the First Amendment.

(1) **freedom** of religion, (2) **freedom** of speech, (3) **freedom** of the press, (4) **the right** to assemble, and (5) **the right** to petition the government.

The freedoms our country was built on did not begin fairly or honestly for all people. It was a long and winding road to get there. In fact, it was brutal. The 1600s brought England to Virginia's shores, and individual colonists and an English King acquired the land rights, treasury rights, and militia rights. America's most tremendous asset at the time was its 3.8 million miles of land. Any land rights of Native Americans were dismissed.

We began as an agrarian society built on private land ownership and enslaved Americans, and so the prosperous American plantation was born. Cotton became such an essential commodity farmed from America's vast land resources that cotton drove the rise of industry and banking. From the time of the American Revolution to the Civil War,

American capitalism was born, and rose to rapid prominence on the backs of enslaved people. Slavery is such a contradiction to American ideals, and it became an inconvenient truth.

How did our country accept the practice of slavery when it was so contrary to its ideals of freedom? The majority put human worth and liberty for all above southern profitability. Post-American Revolution and the War of 1812, we shifted from a declared nationalism to patriotism as a nation. The American patriot was a divided symbol with a galvanized population dedicated to human rights for all, pitted against an agitated population firm in their resolve to affirm States Rights' and the perpetuation of slavery. The rights we valued as a nation reignited the injustice and inhumanity of enslaving human beings and became a significant catalyst for the American Civil War. After the most considerable loss of human life on American soil—roughly 750,000 people— slavery was finally abolished in 1865.

Freedoms advanced again in 1870 with the adoption of the 15th Amendment to the U.S. Constitution, which states, *"The right of citizens of the United States to vote shall not be denied or abridged by the United States or by any State on account of race, color, or previous condition of servitude."* It was not until the 19th Amendment to the U.S. Constitution was ratified in 1920 that American women fought for, and won, the right to vote. The Indian Citizen Act was not passed until 1924, granting citizenship to Native Americans, so that they finally had voting rights. The Voting Rights Act of 1965 strongly prohibits racial discrimination in voting and subsequently increased voting by African American women and men. And finally, just to cement the reality of how many decades and centuries it took to recognize voting rights for all citizens, whether male, female and regardless of race: In <u>1984</u>, Mississippi became the last state in the union to <u>officially</u> ratify the 19th Amendment. The right to vote is an outgrowth of the 1st Amendment Freedoms, but it took from 1789 to 1965--<u>176 years</u>—for Americans to make clear who was considered a voting citizen. The U.S. was in a unique position in that most of our "colonial" citizenry came from aristocratic countries. We had the daunting task of deciding what a democracy should look like, void of any monarchic rule.

Our history is fraught with human rights violations that the 21st century would never tolerate, and yet, in another time—this was not unusual. Young America pushed forward—we developed our patrimony born of American heroes and opportunities to drive, to create, to imagine, and to manifest one's destiny. The American concept of freedom and individuality embodied ideas that had never been accomplished anywhere on Earth. Betsy Ross and the American flag both became symbols of the American Revolution and the young republic. Patrick Henry's famous speech, "Give me liberty or give me death..." became the rallying cry to organize, fortify and defend Virginia from the British.

Our Founding Fathers signed the Declaration of Independence, freeing the American colonies from tyranny. This blueprint of our national ideals became the symbol of American freedom. As men of intellect, invention, politicians at home, and abroad, Benjamin Franklin and Thomas Jefferson became new symbols of American ingenuity, diverse thinking, and diplomacy. Harriet Tubman was a great American hero, who exemplified supreme risk and bravery as she facilitated the transportation of enslaved Americans north to freedom through the

Underground Railroad. As America became an industrial powerhouse, capitalist icons such as Henry Ford, William Randolph Hearst, J.D. Rockefeller, and Cornelius Vanderbilt held monopolies on shipping and railroads, automobiles, and newspapers, epitomizing American commitment to rising industry and progress.

Great military leaders such as George Washington, Ulysses S. Grant, Douglas MacArthur, George Patton, and Dwight Eisenhower protected our country and protected other countries worldwide through alliances. They all embodied the values and vision of American commitment to liberation at home and abroad. The American Civil and World Wars motivated Americans to support our troops, dig in and become a part of the war effort at home, and serve as a daily reminder of how precious those freedoms were to us and to other countries whose freedoms were in peril.

Brilliant scientists and inventors who brought innovation and progress to the world, such as Thomas Edison, Alexander Graham Bell, and Philo Farnsworth, represented the remarkable levels of individual achievement when given the freedom to create. Their innovations in electric power, sound recording, the telephone, and the television marked a new era in mass communication and efficiencies, increasing the American level of comfort, the awareness of the potential, and the inspiration to create. American universities became the best in the world and highly sought after as institutions of learning, working, and teaching. The prize of freedom, the ability to pursue our individuality, and the opportunity to create our own successes became hallmarks of the American Dream and emblems of our American patriotism.

James Truslow Adams' 1931 book, Epic of America, universalized the phrase "American Dream:"

> ... there has been also the American dream, that dream of a
> land in which life should be better and richer and fuller for
> every man, with opportunity for each according to his ability
> or achievement. It is a difficult dream for the European upper
> classes to interpret adequately, and too many of us ourselves
> have grown weary and mistrustful of it. It is not a dream of
> motor cars and high wages merely, but a dream of social order
> in which each man and each woman shall be able to attain
> to the fullest stature of which they are innately capable, and
> be recognized by others for what they are, regardless of the
> fortuitous circumstances of birth or position...The American
> dream that has lured tens of millions of all nations to our
> shores in the past century has not been a dream of merely
> material plenty, though that has doubtlessly counted heav-
> ily. It has been much more than that. It has been a dream of
> being able to grow to fullest development as man and woman,
> unhampered by the barriers, which had slowly been erected
> in the older civilizations, unrepressed by social orders which
> had developed for the benefit of classes rather than for the
> simple human being of any and every class.

When looking at history, American patriotism developed with an almost tunnel-like focus for the first century and a half of our country's existence. We poured our energies into freedoms, industry, and economic power. We became the best at whatever we set our minds. A middle class emerged that became the backbone of the U.S. economy and politics. We protected our country as well as others. We became the world's police force, protecting human life and human rights around the world. We were strong in American symbolism and pride. Made in America!

And then the 1960s happened, and our-roll-up-our-sleeves, tunnel-focused patriotism was turned on its side. The last 50 years of American history have spawned a consistent change in our patriotic dynamic from tunnel patriotism to fluid patriotism. A paradigm shift took shape in the 1960s as we began to move away from the rote and stylized moral duty patriotism of the 1930s to the late 1950s. We embraced a passionate patriotism that cried hypocrisy on our freedoms. That demanded more from a country that was not living up to real justice, real equality, and had a government that was not acting on the will of the people.

Martin Luther King, Jr. brought new clarity to the American Dream and its glaring inequalities in late 1950 and 1960s. His commitment to the Civil Rights Movement challenged lawmakers and citizens to remember that we are all created equal—that no freedoms should be renounced based on color, creed, and religion. The Civil Rights Movement was a determined and organized effort to end racism and enact real racial equality either peacefully or violently. At the same time, the U.S. was involved in the Vietnam War—a war no one wanted, that was heavily criticized and protested. Americans were not invested in Vietnam, in comparison to WWII, either financially or emotionally. Women did not support the war effort in factories, and there were no morale-boosting fireside chats on the household radio. Instead of proudly waving the American flag, this symbol of freedom was seen for the first time on television and in the newspaper, in flames—burning at the hands of angry Americans. The commitment to progress in American society was no longer measured by economic and global strength alone. American society had evolved through historical experience and the changing priorities of a younger generation. We expected more from our national patriotism, we called out injustices within our federal government, as Americans struggled with the need to redefine our national character.

The 1960s brought fluidity to our patriotism and intellectual challenge to our motivations for entering the Vietnam War. The Vietnam War dragged on, with over ten years of American military involvement overlapping two decades, for a fight against Communism that ended with a victory for Communism. The American military draft lowered the average age of American soldiers serving in Vietnam to 21 years old. From 1962 to 1967, we had troops on the ground that grew from around 9,000 to 500,000. Americans read the newspaper each morning; we got in our cars and listened to the news radio, and ended our day watching the news on TV. We saw raw footage televised from the comfort of our own homes each night. It was footage with candid emotion and, sometimes, graphic images. These were not the carefully choreographed newsreels of 1910-1960 shown during previews at the local theatre's Friday night film. It was a tenuous time in American history and culture. As a global superpower, the U.S. aided in the fight for other countries' freedoms in World War I and again in World War II. We were entering a period of the Cold War, and Communism became a genuine threat to our American way of life. The Soviet Union and China were supporting North Vietnam along with other smaller Communist countries. Our concerns at home and abroad were significant. The Soviet Union was a substantial force in destroying Nazi Germany in WWII. The Soviet Union had a will and determination, not unlike the United States. The Cuban Missile Crisis brought a gripping fear of imminent war and Communist takeover into American living rooms for almost two weeks in October 1962. The country waited and watched as world leaders negotiated a "stand down" that could have had disastrous consequences.

The 1970s brought more change and conflict, as our country processed the enormity of the Watergate scandal and deception at the highest level of a government office. The scandal created a rip current in an already changing tide of American patriotism. Lack of trust and a self-serving culture began to fray our patriotic fiber. Americans wrestled with finding an appropriate self-correction to guide the country back to the return of national pride and a rebranded 20th-century conservatism. The Five Freedoms of the 1st Amendment were deployed loudly and proudly for public debate. Growing populations of Americans from diverse demographics were confronted with the realization that the American way of life was changing. We were shedding our innocence. We were challenging our allegiance and our culture and our heritage along with it.

Our current events replay different iterations of 50 years of a changing cultural tide in the US. American freedoms guarantee that we should have the right to debate differing opinions on issues. We tread through dangerous territory when blurred lines exist where freedoms apply to some and not all. We continue to repeat historical failures in a country built on freedoms that have become so intolerant of other's opinions. Our younger generations enrolled in higher learning institutions are unable to gather in an auditorium to listen to a speaker of their choice without fear of reprisal. Our neighbors are afraid to discuss their opinions on any matter related to our beloved country without the fear of abandoned friendship.

Simply put---we are turning on each other concerning issues that revolve around all of these freedoms. We have blindly oppressed the freedoms of religion, speech, the press, the right to assemble, and the right to petition the government in our own country. We have not stood still long enough to reflect on the magnitude of what is transpiring here: the unraveling of First Amendment freedoms in a country that initiated them on the global map.

We live in a world today that makes it very easy for us to move and travel around this big blue marble. Go out and see it! Experiencing other cultures will give you a different perspective on how we live as Americans, good or bad, and how others live. What is their patrimony, their cultural and social essence? We are very judgmental of societies that practice citizen oppression, and yet…

Wake up call. We are doing the same thing to our fellow Americans. Every time someone harasses another human being for their religious persuasion, for their right to express opinions and assemble in groups, we oppress our own society's First Amendment rights. America has a very real and current history of white supremacy that targets American Jews, Muslims, and African Americans. We continue to ignore racial injustice in America. We have groups of American activists that verbally and physically abuse those who attempt to speak on any political topic that is divergent from their agenda—that is not our

American patrimony—that does not honor freedom of speech and the right to assemble. Our institutions of higher learning are supposed to be bastions of free and unoppressed thought; they have become places where many are afraid to express their views and opinions for fear of retaliation and judgment. This viral rise to the violent and angry judgment that drives people to live closeted with their beliefs is no different than someone who struggles with revealing their sexual orientation for fear of violent response and societal perception. It is something to think about when put in those terms, isn't it?

There is a steady stream of antagonistic, hateful language running through our country and concurrently around the world. People of intellect and in positions of leadership—and I am speaking of all parties, as caustic rhetoric knows no boundaries—are lowering the bar when it comes to communicating with others respectfully and with emotional intelligence. This rhetoric is not a carefully crafted message or narrative designed to educate respectfully. It is language designed to elicit anger-induced adrenaline. Sensationalized rhetoric drives information with a sponsored agenda. It seeks to emotionally alarm the public with divisive and often unsubstantiated information, rather than releasing factual data to enable society to draw their own conclusions. It is a form of intentional emotional chaos—look over here, not there—that is undermining our culture. This cycle of hatred has spilled over into businesses, neighborhoods, and schools. Decorum has left the building.

Hatred changes a society of positive, forward-thinking people motivated by ideals of love and acceptance into reactive purveyors of negativity that destroy civilized nations. That is NOT our American patrimony. Negative rhetoric is a manifestation of the Lemming Effect:

it is the dumbing down of Americans when we accept misinformation as the truth even after irrefutable evidence has been presented. If our American patrimony is stripped down to the Framer's architecture for democracy, our American core is based on individual freedoms that promote a positive, inclusive, intelligent, and tolerant society. That is our American patrimony. The real American patrimony has, from the very beginning, been a culture committed to retooling society. We did it with the Declaration of Independence. We recognized the need for a written constitution and gave the Articles of Confederation a try until the U.S. Constitution provided an improved structure for a better democracy. We retooled again with the Bill of Rights and again with Amendments to the Constitution. Our American patriotism carries a responsibility to our nation. We need to own the truth of what our American freedoms have represented, which include our frailties and our failures. Americans owe it to the integrity and perpetuation of American society. We owe the truth to those countries who wish to model American democracy. The American Idea, our American patriotism, is uniquely ours in history, but it has become an idea that belongs to any country wanting the liberties granted by democracy.

CHAPTER 3

An American Mission Statement

American culture has long been referred to as an *idea*: the American Ideal and the American Dream. Seriously thoughtful intention gave form to that *idea* with the framing of the Declaration of Independence. Americans are too removed by time and the comforts of prosperity to conceive of the tremendous efforts involved in this document's architecture. Our young republic consisted of approximately 2.5 million people living in 13 colonies in 1776, the same size as the present-day Kansas state. This young republic of ours had just won a hard-fought war against the most powerful country in the world, Great Britain. Remember, too, American colonists essentially broke the mold when separating from their sovereign country. The civilized world, as it was known, was ruled by monarchies. The colonists' effort was groundbreaking. Our Founders knew that the success of this monumental endeavor must be well-crafted in a signed document that would make it clear to the civilized world that our intentions in separating from England were legitimate and unyielding.

Breaking from tyranny afforded the U.S. a *tabula rasa*, a blank slate. Other countries living under the burdens of oppression and aristocratic societies during the Enlightenment Era were still philosophizing about a "new order." They had not yet acted on the ideals that the U.S. was boldly adopting and implementing without compromise. The American Idea washed ashore from the tidal wave of European Enlightenment that influenced most of 18th-century Europe. This time in European history is vital to understand American history, as this era guided how our Founders developed our government and our way of life. Europe was the civilized world. Through centuries, they had evolved from the Middle Ages to the Age of Discovery (The New World) to the Protestant Reformation (Religious Conflict) to the Renaissance (Art and Aristocratic Opulence) to the Enlightenment (The Age of Reason). This span of approximately 1,000 years had one thing in common: tyranny and oppression in religion, politics, and monarchial rule. After the Renaissance boom in the arts, culture, science, and learning, the next progression brought enlightenment and reason.

The Enlightenment was a period of individualism, intellectual reasoning, and the challenge of the religious and political establishment. This was the age of Englishman Thomas Hobbes and his book Leviathan, which influentially illustrated the formulation of the *social contract theory. The social contract* examined free will absent of any political order; instead, a person's actions are bound only by his or her power and conscience. Hobbes asked why a rational individual would voluntarily consent to give up his or her natural freedom to obtain the benefits of political order. The theory submits that law and political order are not natural elements. It is a human creation, and holds merit because law and political order create a balanced system so that individual freedoms are subjected to the laws of keeping society safe and prosperous. The trick is the balance, as referenced in a cautionary quote from Benjamin Franklin, *"Any society that would give up a little liberty to gain a little security will deserve neither and lose both."*

John Locke wrote several essays that gave wings to the Declaration of Independence. "A Letter Concerning Toleration" spoke to religious tolerance in the wake of a rising tide of Catholicism, and "An Essay Concerning Human Understanding" illuminated the formation of the individual through experience, and natural rights, that all men are born equal. Locke's treatment of *tabula rasa*, while not a new concept, emphasized that the human mind is a 'blank slate" without rules for processing data at birth. Data is introduced to the brain and standards for processes in that data form with human experience. Locke argued that *tabula rasa* meant that the mind of the individual was born blank, and that blank slate was <u>the freedom of the individual to "author" his or her own soul</u>.

The Enlightenment period saw the emergence of what could be called the original bohemians, with the courage of their convictions, rallying a subversive cry for tolerance, change, and freedom from tyranny. The Enlightenment was the beginning of small "meetings" in coffee houses, literary salons, and newspapers where ideas were circulated. These gatherings and exchanges of ideas stirred the pot and sowed the seeds for actualizing meaningful change. The American colonists wanted progressive change, not just philosophical ideology.

Thomas Paine, an English-born American revolutionary, took Locke's ideas a step further and used Locke's principles to engage American colonists with detailed, persuasive arguments in support of freedom from Great Britain. Paine's Common Sense was a brilliant pamphlet published in January of 1776 detailing why the colonies needed to be independent of Great Britain and what our government should look like: a democratic republic. Common Sense was an instant bestseller. By June of 1776, Paine had sold 120,000 copies. That is an enormous number considering that the colonies were a population of approximately 2.5 million people. Common Sense gave Thomas Jefferson a considerable boost in bringing the Declaration of Independence to fruition. The pamphlet's popularity proved that the colonies were solidly behind independence from Great Britain, and it laid out a very straightforward plan for how to accomplish independence.

Remember, the Declaration of Independence was not an end to the American Revolution. July 4, 1776, did not mark the conclusion of the war by any stretch. To that point, George Washington's signature is not on the Declaration because he was in New York, defending Manhattan from the British. The colonies endured the hardships of this war until 1783, almost seven years later. This document was not a treaty—it was a mission statement for independence and the creation of a new republic. Thomas Jefferson was tasked with writing the document, and men like Benjamin Franklin, John Adams, Robert Livingston, and Roger Sherman edited the document. Fifty-six delegates within the 13 colonies signed the Declaration. It was an awe-inspiring time when a war that could have presented insurmountable obstacles for a young, 'understaffed' country became an impassioned battle cry backed with convincing reason and intellect, resulting in the birth of the American Idea.

The Preamble of the Declaration of Independence is a sort of mission statement describing how the colonists felt people should be treated, and why formalizing our intent was necessary to declare independence from England—in writing.

"We hold these truths to be self-evident, that all men are created equal, that they are endowed by their Creator with certain unalienable Rights, that among these are Life, Liberty and the pursuit of Happiness. That to secure these rights, Governments are instituted among Men, deriving their just powers from the consent of the governed."

People are entitled to the fundamental rights of life, freedom, and the pursuit of happiness. Governments exist to protect those rights for the people, and governments are given their power by the people who elect them. People have the right to change or replace a corrupt government; however, making those changes must be of high merit and not based on insignificant issues.

The Declaration of Independence ends with the American colonies stating that this Declaration is based on withstanding years of abusive and corrupted power at the hands of Great Britain. Therefore, the colonists were within their rights to overthrow the British government and establish their own government in its place.

The document then lists all of the ways in which the British King abused his power:

- Freedom of movement was restricted by quartering large numbers of armed troops among the colonists, virtually martial law

- sanctions on colonial trading with all parts of the world, leaving the colonial economy hamstrung and dependent

- Levying taxes on colonies without their consent, and without any representation in government, hurting the local economy and only benefiting Great Britain

- Depriving colonists of the benefits of, and right to a trial by jury

The Declaration of Independence, the American mission statement, extolls equal rights for all humanity and what these rights represent to America. The document is a masterpiece in persuasive argument. But let's be clear, mankind at that time referred to white males only. The signing of the Declaration of Independence was a victory against Great Britain, and with it came the importance of establishing the concrete terms of democracy. America had the attention of the entire Western Hemisphere. The main objectives of the American Idea found form in the 1787 Constitution. Every American citizen should remember the power of these terms: they were designed to keep the power with, and serve the People.

Limited Government: Americans wanted a governing body that was not a monarchy. We wanted the citizenry to enjoy their individual freedoms, and that meant limited government could not dictate a person's occupation, religion, land ownership, etc. Essentially "Life, Liberty and the Pursuit of Happiness" are a God-given right and cannot be dictated by government.

<u>Political Power comes from the People</u>: English philosopher John Locke was very influential during the American Revolution. American founders embraced his philosophy of government as a social contract and advocated for it as a foundation for the American Idea. Citizens vote, and citizens determine what the government and its laws will be. The power of our citizenry is declared in the first three words of the Constitution, *"We the people ..."* This principle is also the foundation of the Declaration of Independence, *"governments are instituted among men, deriving their just powers from the consent of the governed. That whenever any form of government becomes destructive to these ends, it is the right of the people to alter or to abolish it, and to institute new government, laying its foundation on such principles and organizing its powers in such form, as to them shall seem most likely to affect their safety and happiness."*

<u>A Limited Representative Republic</u>: Our Founders' intentions and beliefs were that limited government formed as a representative republic was the People's best opportunity to have a just and free society. Anything less, such as a direct democracy where individuals vote on every issue rather than on an elected representative, would result in chaos or mob rule. The thinking was that any system allowing special interests ultimately gained control of the country. Our Founders took measures to protect against government oppression through the dispersal of power. Under the Constitution, each branch of government can check on

every other department of government's authority. These branches cascade to the state level in terms of checks and balances on the national level.

A Written Contract—the U.S. Constitution: As Americans creating this great society, our Founding Fathers realized that this social contract for the People, by the People needed to be formally written and ratified. Thomas Paine, whose brilliance brought us Common Sense and gave wings to the Declaration of Independence, wrote, *"[A]n unwritten constitution is not a constitution at all."* We may take this piece of our heritage's beginnings for granted. The idea of the Constitution is so indelibly etched in American minds, but remember—at the time this was written, England was THE most powerful country on the face of the Earth—and they had no written constitution.

Private Property Rights: The right to private property was synonymous with freedoms and liberty in the minds of our Founders. Actualized freedoms, as they were intended, would never permit the government to possess a person's property, unless you were Black, or a woman or a Native American. James Madison said, "As a man is said to have a right to his property, he may be equally said to have a property in his rights."

American perseverance and commitment to freedom was and is an ongoing endeavor. The colonial delegates were continually tweaking the American framework. In 1791, we took the Constitution a step further by defining the Bill of Rights:

Amendment 1

Freedom of Religion, Speech, and the Press

The First Amendment guarantees freedoms concerning religion, expression, assembly, and the right to petition. It forbids Congress from both promoting one religion over others and also restricting an individual's religious practices. It guarantees freedom of expression by prohibiting Congress from restricting the press or allowing individuals to speak freely. It also ensures the right of citizens to assemble peaceably and to petition their government.

Amendment 2

The Right to Bear Arms

The Second Amendment protects the individual right to possess a firearm unconnected with service in the militia, and to use that firearm for traditionally lawful purposes, such as self-defense within the home.

Amendment 3

The Housing of Soldiers

The Third Amendment forbids the forcible housing of military personnel in a citizen's home during peacetime and requires the process to be "prescribed by law" in times of war.

Amendment 4

Protection from Unreasonable Searches and Seizures

The Fourth Amendment initially enforced the notion that "each man's home is his castle," secure from unreasonable searches and property seizure by the government. It protects against arbitrary arrests and is the basis of the law regarding search warrants, wiretaps, and other forms of surveillance.

Amendment 5

Protection of Rights to Life, Liberty, and Property

The Fifth Amendment provides for several rights regarding criminal and civil legal proceedings. It guarantees the right to a grand jury and protects against self-incrimination. It also requires that "due process of law" be a part of any proceeding that denies a citizen "life, liberty, or property" and requires the government to compensate citizens when it takes private property for public use.

Amendment 6

Rights of Accused Persons in Criminal Cases

The Sixth Amendment guarantees the rights of criminal defendants, including the right to a public trial without unnecessary delay, the right to a lawyer, the right to an impartial jury, and the right to know who your accusers are and the nature of the charges and evidence against you.

Amendment 7

Rights in Civil Cases

The Seventh Amendment distinguishes civil claims in federal civil court, which must be tried before a jury, from claims and issues that may be heard by a judge alone.

Amendment 8

Excessive Bail, Fines, and Punishments Forbidden

The Eighth Amendment prohibits cruel and unusual punishments, excessive fines, and bail, in conjunction with incarceration.

Amendment 9

Other Rights Kept by the People

The Ninth Amendment was James Madison's attempt to ensure that the Bill of Rights was not seen as granting to the people of the United States, only the specific rights are addressed. It was a kind of insurance policy to address that there were unquantified rights outside of those stated explicitly in the Bill of Rights.

Amendment 10

Undelegated Powers Kept by the States and the People

The Tenth Amendment helps to define the relationship between Federal and State governments. This addresses the issue of reconciling state and national interests as they apply to the Federal powers to tax, police, and regulate.

After signing the Declaration of Independence in July 1776, it took 11 years, at the 1787 Constitutional Convention when our Founding Fathers gathered to develop a document that the country could live by. The Declaration of Independence was not ultimately ratified by the states until two years later, in 1789. The transition from a monarchy to a republic and a democracy took time. All the players involved desired a quality document with intention, purpose, and reason. This was not arbitrarily decided in a Tweet or a Facebook post. Today, our lightning speed technology and exchange of information have many positives in sharing ideas, images, and knowledge. The downside of technology is that it has created a population of emotional reactors rather than thoughtful contributors.

There is always debate, worldwide, on whether the framing doctrine of religion or nation can stand the test of time. Religious documents from the Qu'ran to the Holy Bible have long been debated on their arcane language and ideas regarding women and LGBT people, whose rights the world has been slower to address. As we evolve as a society, individual pieces of any doctrine no longer make sense in terms of the commitment to humanity and dignity. Would it not be accurate and inclusive if the Declaration of Independence read, "…all humankind are created equal" instead of "mankind?" We left out the female sex. The language only referred to white men. I am getting into the weeds for a reason. The language applied to the times. The interpretation has intelligently evolved through the thoughtful guidance of the Supreme Court and others studying constitutional law.

As a country committed to freedoms, we recognized that amendments to the U.S. Constitution that go beyond the original Bill of Rights were necessary. The 13th Amendment abolished slavery and involuntary servitude, except as a punishment for a crime. The 15th Amendment provided that all male American citizens should be allowed to vote and not be denied based on color, race, or previous condition of servitude. The 19th Amendment granted women, as American citizens, the right to vote.

These amendments provide clarity and definition and the ability for Americans to collectively author and execute ideas for our society that adapt to change, experience, and enlightenment. Almost 250 years later, this country remains a society that values a commitment to inclusive freedoms and fair process through amended laws.

CHAPTER 4

Birth of the American Patriot

History is the framework for our cultural identity. It connects events through time that become our national legacy and defines us as being human. A considerable part of American cultural identity is celebrating the Fourth of July. We celebrate independence and Old Glory as we gather with friends and family. We enjoy our great American traditions: picnicking with hot dogs and apple pie, watching parades, baseball games, and fireworks. These pastimes are part of our cultural heritage. They have become etched in our patrimony. A society's historical past creates and influences its future. However, the Fourth of July loses its meaning when Americans focus only on our pastimes and ignore the magnitude of the history behind the date.

> *"A nation reveals itself not only by the men it produces, but also by the men it honors, the men it remembers"* —President John F. Kennedy, October 1963.

Time, distance, and the loss of our witnesses to history can erode the feelings and the passion that inspires us. We have an incredibly successful country, and generation after generation forgets what it took to get us there. It is a challenge that requires significant commitment to keep these stories alive for future generations. Heroes are a genuine inspiration and reminder of what great deeds and character look like.

By 1800, most of our Revolutionary War heroes were gone—but the stories were still fresh for the children of that generation. When the Civil War came and went in the 1860s, the very last of those veterans were still living in the 1950s, a man named Albert Henry Woolson (1850-1956). Americans had new war heroes from the 1860s onward as we continued to become involved in wars for freedom from oppression throughout the world. According to the Department of Veterans Affairs, of the 16 million veterans who served in WWII, less than 2% of those veterans are still alive today. We lose roughly 300 WWII veterans a day, and the younger segment of this group is in their early nineties. The American War Library estimates that approximately one-third of those who served in Vietnam are alive today.

The heroes who protected freedom and democracy during times of American-involved conflict are disappearing from our Independence Day parades, celebrations that continue because these heroes inspire us. They remind us of our country's commitment to freedom, and they symbolize the human sacrifice and bravery that grants our society the privileges we enjoy daily. Most American citizens have not known and will never know what it would be like to live any other way. This is why it is essential to understand our history because history is more than just dates and events.

Grade school history generally focuses on memorizing facts. As we get older and develop more emotional maturity, we become able to process history to help us make sense of the past. What were the original intentions in these historical events, and what circumstances led to specific outcomes? It is not as simple as opposing teams with one winner and one loser. What tipped the balance? Understanding history's lessons are what makes us human because, in hindsight, we can explore our human frailties. Hopefully, the human mind can reason that history provides lessons: that power corrupts, that human beings have free will, and that perspective ultimately rests at the doorstep of cause and effect.

Empirical Colonies

This country began as a wild, new world with a small population and challenges that slowed progress. Today, our American population is almost 300,000 times larger than it was 350 years ago. Eras of growth are now measured in mere decades—or less—as opposed to periods in history used to measure progress over a century. It is hard to imagine, and essential to remember, that exploration and colonization of America took place over 270 years. The American colonies were populated by European pilgrims and settlers who, in the name of their monarchs, contracted to colonize the New World. European countries were competing to colonize new land, rich in natural resources, to increase trade, commerce, wealth, and empires.

Both Great Britain and France also sent convicts abroad to the American colonies. "Transportation" was typically the term used to refer to the commuted sentence for a convict sent abroad. Exile became a popular European alternative to the severe punishment of a death sentence for a felony charge. Instead, convicts were frequently sent to the American colonies to serve their prison term in penal colonies.

The prison system solved a variety of problems for countries such as England and France. The correctional institution provided a lesser sentence commensurate with the felony charge, it decreased the over-crowded prisons in both countries, and it cleansed cities and towns of an "undesirable element."

Penal colonies generated an income to offset the cost of maintaining them by allowing the English or the French to sell the released convict into indentured servitude to a wealthy colonist. This approach benefited the origin country by keeping the convict in the colonies and leaving that person without the means to return to Europe. Additionally, those who were not Catholics or followers of the Church of England could 'relocate' to the colonies to freely practice their religions, as they were not welcome in most of Western Europe.

The natural resources in America were so highly prized that Europe's hands were entirely on the pulse of every operation in the colonies. Prosperity was envisioned by both the King of England and the free people who came to the colonies. However, the King was still the colonial sovereign, and success came at a price—via tariffs and alle-giance. The reality was that military forts and local militias populated the colonies to serve the King, protect the interests of the King in the colonies, and ensure a just society per the laws decreed by the King of England. The colonies were a large, prosperous trading post, and service to the monarchy was England's intention for the American colonies.

There was a multitude of problems with England's arrangement. The original inhabitants of the New World were pushed out and regarded as savages. England brought self-proclaimed land entitlement and disease to the Native American tribes. Angry Native Americans fought to protect their lands, their heritage, and their people. Adversaries England and France battled along with colonists and Native Americans. Colonists were working hard in a new world of abundant resources, but they were taxed at an absurd level, leaving meager profits for the individual. Freedom was mostly background noise during these early years, overshadowed by power and control—oppression and taxation. The drumbeat of liberty and the American Revolution became the seed of hope in every city and village until angry, oppressed colonists' motivation for change took center stage.

The American Revolution and the Declaration of Independence were the demarcation line for change from a world of tyranny, oppression, and sovereign rule to a world of freedom with a self-ruling government and a written constitution. Independence was certainly not the vision aristocratic and empirical Great Britain had for the colonies. For the colonies to achieve independence, civilians required enough time and oppressive circumstances to reach the tipping point. Two hundred seventy years passed before the colonies arrived at the dawn of the American Revolution, and another 26 years passed to gain independence from England.

The Articles of Confederation

A decade passed from the time of the signing of the Declaration of Independence to the development of an agreed-upon document that detailed democracy and truly reflected the blueprint for the young republic: the U.S. Constitution. However, the Articles of Confederation have a prominent place in that historical context and became a major catalyst for the coming Constitution. The Articles were an early attempt to unionize the colonies with less national and more state government. The states had greater autonomy. Under the Articles, the colonies were established as the "United States of America." A union of these states was formed to defend the states as a whole. There were weaknesses throughout the document that did not allow for a cohesive government and gave more control to the states; the Articles hamstrung government process—and progress.

For example, the Articles did not allow for oversight with an executive branch and a judicial branch of the central government. It required an unrealistic 9 of 13 majority votes to pass any legislation within the 13 states. To add to the subject of congressional voting, the Articles made any amendments almost impossible to ratify. Those proposed amendments would require a <u>unanimous</u> vote from a constituency of very different states that had very different priorities. Each state had its own monetary system, which made trade between states and other nations extremely difficult. The provisions in the Articles rendered centralized government ineffective in matters of foreign policy. The lack of definition of central government powers to enforce international law gave the states individual autonomy to determine and interpret foreign policy as they saw fit.

Finally, the mounting post-revolutionary war debts owed to France and the Netherlands were compromised by the lack of a unified monetary system between states and a central government without the power to tax those states. All of these factors left the "United States" with a large fiscal deficit and an ineffective government system. The Articles of

Confederation were an experiment in democracy that required a more substantial commitment to detailed parameters. It asked Congress and its constituency to trust and relinquish some powers to a centralized government at a time when Americans were fresh off the battlefield of war against sovereignty.

The Articles of Confederation, as a precursor to the U.S. Constitution, have a unique place in history with a relevance to the present day. Is there a developing path for redirecting the balance of power between national and state governments? 2020 has shown a spotlight on over a half-century of ineffective leadership within state government illustrated by the handling of the COVID pandemic and the decay of urban law and order. Significant state autonomy is important to the balance of power measured against the national government in the democracy outlined in the U.S. Constitution.

How has the ability for states to individually ratify amendments, such as the 19th Amendment, contributed to the perpetuation of systemic racism and inequality? The 19th Amendment, giving women the right to vote, was proposed by Congress in 1878. It finally passed through the House in 1919, and the last state to ratify the 19th Amendment was Mississippi in 1984. Almost 100 years of inefficient government process to ratify an Amendment for equality.

The 1787 Constitutional Convention Revisited and Abridged

It is May 1787, and delegates are gathering in Philadelphia to discuss the flaws of the Articles of Confederation, one major issue being the inefficiency of a diminished national government. At a minimum, there is an agreement that the necessity exists to frame a Constitution that protects individuals' freedoms while providing for a fair, balanced, and limited government. The Constitution would organize a system for the national government that puts the power in the hands of the people and consists of several branches establishing a checks and balances system.

This U.S. Constitution is an experiment in creating a fair democracy. Not all Americans are on board with the ideas framing the Constitution. Those supporting the ratification of the Constitution are in favor of a more defined national republic. These citizens are known as Federalists. Prominent Federalists include John Adams, Alexander Hamilton, John Jay, and James Madison. Those who opposed the ratification of the Constitution in favor of small localized government are known as Anti-Federalists. They are the original states' rights advocates and are concerned with a single government entity's authority over local state issues. Prominent Anti-Federalists include Patrick Henry, Thomas Jefferson, and Samuel Adams.

After months of drafts and rewrites, the Constitution is approved by the majority vote in September 1787. It must go through ratification by each of the 13 states. Opposition to ratifying the Constitution is strong in the state of New York. After the document is adopted by delegation, Anti-Federalists begin publishing newspaper articles criticizing it. The argument opposing the document is that, as written, it gives Congress an excess of power. There is potential for the American people to lose the liberties they fought for in the American Revolution. As you can imagine, this is an incredibly emotional issue, after fighting for freedoms for almost 20 years, and at a time when the war had only ended four years prior.

There is a commitment to developing a clear path to individual freedoms within a strong national system governed by the people. During the debate of the Constitution's ratification is when a few prominent American patriots begin to author a series of anonymously published essays to argue in favor of the Constitution's ratification.

Publius

Publius Valerius Poplicola, a 5th century B.C. Roman leader who headed the overthrow of a monarchial rule that led to the establishment of the first Roman Republic, was the inspiration for the pen name for the *Federalist Papers*. A series of 85 essays were published by 'Publius,' with over 50 of these essays written by a tireless Alexander Hamilton, a few by John Jay, and the rest by James Madison. The published articles were created to answer questions and educate New Yorkers on the proposed U.S. Constitution and rally voters to ratify the Constitution in New York.

Among the most noted *Federalist Papers*, *Federalist No. 1*, Hamilton addressed the debate over the ratification of the Constitution and "whether societies of men are really capable or not of establishing good government from reflection and choice, or whether they are forever destined to depend for their political constitutions on accident and force." In response to critics of the Constitution arguing that the "proposed" federal government was too large, unwieldy, and unresponsive to the people, James Madison wrote an essay exploring it. In

Federalist No. 10, he argued that tyranny would be avoided with the formation of groups that, under the law, would be compelled to negotiate, compromise, and find agreeable solutions under the challenges of a diverse constituency. In *Federalist* No. *51*, James Madison explains and defends the checks and balances system in the Constitution. He further elaborates on how the Republican government can serve as a check on the power of factions and the majority's tyranny.

We have all most likely heard more about the impeachment process, and the arguments for and against impeachment, in recent history than we care. Many of us have lived the history that speaks to *Federalist No. 66*. We have witnessed the impeachment of two U.S. Presidents and the resignation of one under the scrutiny of impeachment, all three within the last 50 years. The importance of *Federalist No.66* is this: impeachment was not a judicial process set in place to be used as a tool to oust an elected official by an opposing political party because of differences in approach to governing. It was heavily debated in 2019-20 during the Trump impeachment hearings, and it fell under perjury for Clinton in terms of his personal life.

Alexander Hamilton's argument in *Federalist No. 66* rebukes Anti-Federalist discussions regarding the Senate having the power as the impeachment court and the Senate's potential to overreach its authority and infringe on the Judicial Branch. Hamilton states that giving the Senate this specific judicial power prevents potentially substantial abuses and provides the check and balance power to the Legislative Branch concerning the Executive Branch. In response to the Senate possibly gaining too much power and running the government, Hamilton defends the Constitution by arguing that the House of

Representatives, as the larger entity of the Legislative Branch, predominates the Senate with its exclusive powers to move to impeach. The last piece of Hamilton's argument in response to the Senate's ability to impartially judge is that the Senate must rely on "evidences of guilt so extraordinary."

Why are the Federalist Papers important? They are one of the most crucial persuasive argument documents after the Declaration of Independence. They were written with tireless commitment (85 essays) to defend an equitable approach to government within a democracy. Just as importantly, they were written with respect for human beings, their freedoms, and the intelligence to understand human nature and the lure of power.

CHAPTER 5

The Young Republic

The War of 1812 brought international trade into the picture for the young American Republic. While Great Britain and France were at war with each other, each country tried to block the United States from trading with the other. The British were also gaining notoriety for pirating American merchant ships at sea and forcing them to serve for the British Royal Navy, which was suffering workforce shortages. American expansion substantially increased abundant natural resources, and with the Louisiana Purchase in 1803, the U.S. became a massive threat to empirical Great Britain. An increasingly prosperous American economy financially independent from England became an international trade force. Additionally, England increased its efforts to regain financial controls and limit American economic growth by supplying Native Americans with firearms to help them achieve an independent state in the Northwest—a subversive attempt to block U.S. expansion.

It was a costly war for Americans, with over $200 million spent on the war effort and a U.S. Navy. Why Americans would put the country through another war only a few short decades after the American

Revolution seems an appropriate question. One of the compelling answers many could argue is that of honor.

> *Americans of every political stripe saw the need to uphold national honor, and to reject the treatment of the United States by Britain as a third class nonentity. Americans talked incessantly about the need for force in response. This quest for honor was a major cause of the war in the sense that most Americans who were not involved in mercantile interests or threatened by Indian attack strongly endorsed the preservation of national honor.* --Bradford Perkins excerpt from The Causes of the War of 1812

There is no question that after hard-fought independence, and with a well-crafted mission statement, American integrity was something to be revered and upheld at any cost. In preserving and protecting any society, prosperity must exist, or society will extinguish itself. The economics of defending our future growth would have played heavily alongside honor. Americans knew what we had, and Europe wanted it. What country would not fight to preserve independent prosperity, knowing their economy and democracy was the envy of others?

England was fighting a war on two fronts. England's army stretched thin created certain advantages for the U.S. The U.S. had moved from militias in favor of an organized U.S. Army and a U.S. Navy that was able to take on England, the most powerful navy in the world in both strength and military strategy. This new and improved military was a pivotal moment for America defending her borders. The significance of the War of 1812 cannot be underestimated. It gave the U.S. what the discovery of fire gave to the caveman. The war elevated the level to which we were capable of protecting ourselves and protecting what had become an American way of life. It forever changed the definition of American patriotism, expanding the concepts of freedom, honor, and resilience to include power and might.

Antebellum America and the American Civil War

This era marked the beginning of a new relationship with England, as peaceful recognition of an independent America afforded amicable ties with the British. The U.S. was able to focus on building a stable country instead of the heightened vigilance required to defend it. The economy began to rebuild after the War of 1812. The U.S. essentially had two economies. The agricultural South generated huge profits with its tobacco and cotton plantations populated with a labor force of enslaved people. The industrial North processed those resources in factories and facilitated commerce through large ports and mercantile banking. As the country prospered economically, new territories increased, and the country expanded westward.

With their busy ports, the Northern states had a steady stream of immigrants arriving to live and work in America. Northerners understood earning a wage or paying a wage earner to perform in a job. Southerners had long prospered under the high-profit margins that slave ownership granted, a way of life, and a labor force that they did not want to change. The problem became what to do with the western states and territories. Should slavery continue in some of those states and not others? Where is the line drawn--or should slavery end altogether?

History can often paint the picture of any victory as a righteous win. While slavery was an institution that should never have happened and needed to end, the Northern Union's demands for freedom of all people and an end to the inhumanity of slavery was not entirely as altruistic as it seemed. Rapid growth gives way to inherent problems. The nation grew from 24 states in the Union, to 34 states within 40 years. During the Constitutional Convention of 1789, the Three-Fifths Compromise enacted legislation that said each slave represented three-fifths of a citizen. This number went toward each state's total population for state representation and taxation purposes. Granting new western territories or states slavery rights would give those states higher numbers and more significant representation in legislation. The Northern states did not want lose power, and the fact that the North included smaller states and "free states" would result in a lesser legislative representation for the Northern states.

After blazing new territory in a new land, the young republic freed the colonies from tyranny. Once the framework for an independent society was created, America built commerce to a desirable level within the Western Hemisphere. After re-engaging Great Britain in a war at sea that gave credence and renowned to an inexperienced U.S. Navy, Americans focused inward. Within 40 years, we were a divided country, fighting a homeland war, with the most significant loss of life in American history.

November 19, 1863

This date should have more significance for the average American than it typically does. Fifteen thousand people gathered at the site of the largest battle of the Civil War, in terms of scale and violence—a battle that had occurred only four months prior. To give perspective to scale, outside of the tremendous number of lives lost: 120 generals were present at the Battle of Gettysburg, nine of whom died because of that battle. Sixty-four Medals of Honor were awarded to Union soldiers for bravery at the Battle of Gettysburg.

The somber scene was a cemetery dedication, intended to be delivered by Edward Everett, a former U.S. Senator, former president of Harvard, and former Secretary of State. As the crowd gathered, they watched as men continued to bury the dead from the battle four months prior. Gettysburg was a sobering moment for the continuance of a young republic of fewer than 100 years, and the hope for its survival. Lincoln was invited to give some very brief remarks, as Everett's speech was the keynote and two hours in duration. Lincoln's address, spoken in fewer than two minutes, is what remains etched in time.

The Great American Legacy in Short Remarks

Four score and seven years ago, our fathers brought forth on this continent, a new nation, conceived in liberty and dedicated to the proposition that all men are created equal. Now we are engaged in a great civil war, testing whether that nation, or any nation so conceived and so dedicated, can long endure. We are met on a great battlefield of that war. We have come to dedicate a portion of that field, as a final resting place for those who here gave their lives that that nation might live. It is altogether fitting and proper that we should do this. But, in a larger sense, we cannot dedicate—we cannot consecrate—we cannot hallow—this ground. The brave men, living and dead, who struggled here, have consecrated it, far above our poor power to add or detract. The world will little note, nor long remember what we say here, but it can never forget what they did here. It is for us the living, rather, to be dedicated here to the unfinished work which they who fought here have thus far so nobly advanced. It is rather for us to be here dedicated to the great task remaining before us—that from these honored dead we take increased devotion to that cause for which they gave the last full measure of devotion—that we here highly resolve that these dead shall not have died in vain—that this nation, under God, shall have a new birth of freedom—and that government of the people, by the people, for the people, shall not perish from the earth.—Abraham Lincoln Gettysburg Address

Lincoln's Gettysburg Address of 257 words has endured for over a century and a half as a document and oration of unity, freedom, and hope for humanity. The impact of which has been embraced globally. The Civil War had a tragic beauty as most civil or homeland wars do. It seems so hard to imagine a country torn in half that it takes up arms to destroy itself for four years with the human toll somewhere between 650,000 to 750,000 lives to fight for human rights and an end to slavery.

These turning points in history show the best in humanity, as they expose its worst.

CHAPTER 6

American Exceptionalism

By the late 1800s, the United States' young country had existed for over 100 years. We had built a nation based on liberty, egalitarianism, individualism, republicanism, and democracy. We had a written Constitution. We won our independence from the most powerful country on earth, not once but twice. We built an Army and Navy to rival Great Britain's so that we would always be able to defend our nation and our way of life. We worked to expand our country, and then abolish a slave institution that afforded a level of commerce, enabling the U.S. to become a formidable trade partner. We began developing our economy beyond agrarianism. We created a strong economy that invited entrepreneurship and innovation. American Exceptionalism became popularized during a time in American history that illustrated a unified democracy's ability to overcome considerable obstacles. We renounced tyranny and sovereignty, which had governed countries for thousands of years, and ended the practice of slavery that had built civilizations for thousands of years. The reforms that defined our country, such as a written Constitution that could be amended to improve civil liberties, became a benchmark for societal change globally. Based on the actions through early American history, the world *reacted* with a wave of democratic revolution from the late 1700s to the present day.

Historical perspective is vastly different from science or math in that there are no finite answers. Lack of perspective can leave many with a considerable degree of uncertainty, intolerance, and stress. Suppose we use historical perspective in a reasonable, thought-provoking way and with a significant degree of balanced emotion. In that case, we can process philosophical thought and the conditions of the time. Perspective is how we gain monumental insight and tolerance for the evolution of society.

Freedoms and equality, regardless of the lapse of time and distance from our nation's formative years, are principles that Americans have remained committed to upholding. Remembering our remarkable history that forged those freedoms is vital to American society. It is crucial to truly understand the astonishing level of sacrifice that our ancestors made to execute that vision, just as we need to understand and accept that humanity is not perfect. We have hopes and dreams for an ideal society, but we also have free will as human beings.

One of the tragedies of humanity is that we become selective on whom those liberties apply to, and not everyone uses their powers for good. The Civil War tore our country in half, left a beleaguered economy, and, most tragically, resulted in the most substantial loss of American life to date. The outcome was the abolition of slavery. This historical event in American history is significant and a turning point for our country. The decision to abolish slavery deserves praise, but Americans were far from the first to remove the practice and, in fact, were among the last countries to do so. The lives that were shackled in servitude for centuries are a dark truth that we, as human beings, should never forget and continue to struggle with centuries later.

An Overlooked American Hero

One of the true heroes of the American Civil War was someone that history does not always revere. An honest account of what Ulysses S. Grant did for our country is not taught in a large portion of American classrooms. I was raised during my early childhood in the South, and then later in the North. During the 1970s and living in Virginia, I was taught the history of the Confederate General Robert E. Lee, not the Union General Grant. I have visited Lee's home atop Arlington Cemetery and walked the grounds of Washington & Lee University, where the Lee family crypt resides—along with Lee's horse Traveller. As a Richmond resident, I have spent the last 15 years driving down Richmond's Monument Avenue, lined with statues of Robert E. Lee, Jeb Stuart, and Jefferson Davis. The South has not forgotten, and these statues are potent symbols that represent a culture from over 150 years ago that still exists. Removing many of these monuments to the "Lost Cause" changes the landscape of Monument Avenue as it creates opportunities to change the culture of systemic racism.

When Americans look to history for courage, honor, respect, vision, and faith in humanity, Union General and U.S. President Grant embodied these core principles. He came from a family that was anti-slavery and married into a Southern family who owned slaves. When Grant worked his farm, Grant worked alongside the slave his father-in-law provided. Grant was extremely uncomfortable with this practice, and he gave that man his respect and dignity by granting his freedom many years before Grant entered the Civil War.

Ulysses S. Grant served with distinction in the Mexican-American War before becoming the Commanding General of the Union Army during the Civil War. He was a devoted husband to his wife, Julia, and his four children. When Confederate General Pemberton surrendered to Grant at Vicksburg, Grant allowed Pemberton, his men, and Vicksburg citizens to keep their personal property—<u>except for slaves</u>. The Confederate South found the suggestion that slaves were not included in personal property oppression of their rights to freely own slaves. Ulysses S. Grant became known as "Unconditional Surrender" Grant. The practice of slavery and slave ownership was nonnegotiable and unacceptable in his mind.

Grant was educated at West Point, and several of the Confederate officers were his classmates. They were on opposing sides, but he gave them the respect and honor of an officer and a soldier. General Grant allowed Confederate soldiers to keep their horses to return home to plow their fields. He encouraged the enlistment of black soldiers in the Union Army. The Union soldier to whom Grant gave the distinction of recording the surrender at Appomattox Courthouse was an American Indian.

When Lincoln was assassinated, Andrew Johnson became President and began dismantling Reconstruction policies. Grant fought tirelessly to reinforce the freed slaves act. He was not a politician but became the next Republican President. He served two terms in an administration that inherited war debt, and he battled to keep Reconstruction at the forefront of American progress for all people. Grant created the Department of Justice and aggressively prosecuted the Klu Klux Klan members of Democratic Confederate veterans. Grant got in and did the hard work of repairing the nation with integrity and determination. His guiding principles were not determined by the direction of the wind and popularity but rather integrity, common sense, and dignity for all people.

With the ratification of the 14th and 15th Amendments, granting citizenship to former slaves and establishing voting rights, African Americans began voting in record numbers. One of the great positives about freedom is the openness to speak your mind and share philosophies and opinions. Empowered freedoms can wield a double-edged sword when the evils of intolerance enter in. A southern faction found workarounds within our society of freedoms for the continuance of oppression. Many could not let go of the end of slavery. This reluctance had little to do with the practice of free labor and servitude, and everything to do with supremacy and control. The Jim Crow Laws became a vehicle for the southern states to perpetuate racial bias from the 1890s until the Civil Rights Movement of the 1960s through a Poll Tax and a Literacy Test. They were enacted by white supremacists bent on legalizing and enforcing racial discrimination. These laws were designed to prevent African Americans from voting, and the laws were successful. During Reconstruction, 90% of African American men were registered to vote. By 1940, only three percent of eligible African American men were registered to vote. Ironically, the South would not let go of the need to control freedoms just as England would not let go of its control of trade and taxation of the U.S. until the War of 1812.

Control and corrupted power are where humanity's dark side enters with new ideas that resurrect old, reviled practices--benefiting some and not all. We need to remember our history—the good and the bad. The good is there to celebrate our achievements and venerate great deeds and people whose tremendous sacrifice gave us the country we are privileged to live in today. It is a privilege and a birthright, but beyond that, we are all accountable for how it moves forward.

All that is Gilded is Not Gold

What has guided change in our American society over the last 150 years? We exited the Civil War and Reconstruction to enter a pivotal time for the American economy, politics, and widespread social reforms. The Gilded Age and the Progressive Era expanded the shape of American Patriotism from freedoms, individuality, and equality to include prosperity, ingenuity, and "American know-how."

The Gilded Age was a time of steroidal growth and expansion for the American economy. American wages surpassed European wages, which resulted in an increased flow of immigrants from Europe who were guided through ports of entry such as Ellis Island. From the 1860s Civil War to the 1890s Gilded Age, we evolved from an agrarian society to dominance in industry and manufacturing. Factory workers' wages increased by over 50% for skilled laborers. American industrialization overtook that of Great Britain's. We were using mostly iron and steel materials to power machines, and we had developed new energy sources and fuels like coal, petroleum, the steam engine, and electricity. It was the beginning of organization in the factories and a new division of labor.

The American railroad industry boomed as transportation became vital to connect our ever-expanding country that crossed east to west, approximately 2,800 miles. The railroad moved the goods and services that the industrial age provided and facilitated, as well as transporting food from the agrarian states to the non-agrarian states. The railroad was a large-scale employer, no matter where you lived in the country.

Institutions of higher learning thrived and expanded as the demand for engineering and managerial expertise increased. Imagine this kind of expansion and growth nationwide without modern communications. Enter the telegraph to wire connection, as efficiently as that era allowed, to link people and share information. The invention of the telephone, the radio, and the phonograph made daily communication viable over vast distances and facilitated the ability to enjoy entertainment and news in your own home. News reached the masses as newspapers and magazines were anticipated each morning and evening like today's latest Instagram feed or Tweet.

Large corporations became the new business organization model and gave birth to the managerial movement and career paths. The Golden Age was a time of industry-led by financial magnates such as Rockefeller, Vanderbilt, Frick, Guggenheim, Flagler, Mellon, Carnegie, and J.P. Morgan, and Wall Street flourished. Just as the American Revolution became the symbol of freedom and individuality, the Gilded Age became the symbol of what Americans could accomplish with the freedom to do so. Reconstruction promised significant change after the Civil War, but the end of slavery and the granting of voting rights were replaced with sharecropping and Jim Crow Laws. Systemic racism was rampant, violent labor strikes raged throughout the country, and political corruption was characteristic of the Gilded Age, as was the great divide between wealth and poverty.

Beloved American author, Mark Twain, coined the name given to the late 19th century to describe the era as a thin golden layer on the surface with corruption lying below. The Gilded Age represented a time of greed, political scandal, and vulgar displays of wealth. It also served as a time in America's "coming of age" when our agrarian society shifted from individual producers and handicrafts to a modern, urban society led by manufacturing and industrial corporations. The Gilded Age produced a modern industrial economy that created wealth beyond imagining. However, it also produced substantial economic disparities and a great political divide.

> *"A person is a person through other persons; you can't be human in isolation; you are human only in relationships"—Bishop Desmond Tutu.*

Human nature is characterized by struggles driven by free will and power, as evidenced throughout world history. If the Gilded Age was the American age of opulence, the Progressive Era saw Americans build a social infrastructure on the foundation of successful capitalism. The Progressive Era championed humanity. It brought the focus back on building relationships within our communities. Wage inequities, corporate monopolies, and social elitism that benefited a minority of the population created a massive wedge in American politics and social behavior until *reform* became the operative word of the day. The Progressive Era, spanning the 1890s to the 1920s, became another American benchmark for the world to emulate.

The Progressive Era was a top-down reform that included breaking up monopolies and regulating banking through the creation of the Federal Reserve System. Andrew Carnegie's philosophy of the wealthy owing a debt to society became an influential model for other wealthy captains of industry. Philanthropy became a trend in wealthy circles as significant individual financial donations benefited libraries, museums, hospitals, research, universities, and religious institutions.

The middle class emerged as a powerful entity, bridging the gap between the upper and working classes. During the Progressive Era, women let the austere mantle of the Victorian Era fall from their shoulders and replaced it with the newfound freedom and equality of the Progressive Era. The divorce rate increased as women's suffrage changed a woman's right to vote and gave American women an empowered voice and freedom outside their homes. Women entered higher education and a skilled workplace. Activism for women's voting rights, child labor laws, social reform, and public health became prominent advocacy.

As Richmond, Virginia has been my home for 15 years; I will use the example of several local Richmonders during the Gilded Age and Progressive Era: businessman Lewis Ginter, his niece, philanthropist Grace Arents, and African American businesswoman and educator Maggie Walker. Lewis Ginter was the son of Dutch immigrant parents who relocated from New York City to Richmond as an adult in 1842. He invested in tobacco and sugar as well as real estate. He served in the military and was present when Robert E. Lee surrendered at Appomattox. Post-war, returning to the fire-ravaged city of Richmond, Lewis Ginter began the business of rebuilding Richmond and forgiving war debts. He surveyed and built the first Richmond suburbs and an electric tramway system. Ginter built a hotel in Richmond, The Jefferson, and the cost in the 1890s was extremely extravagant at five to ten million dollars. The Jefferson Hotel was considered one of the grandest hotels in the country, and it still is a magnificent hotel. Lewis Ginter held one of the largest fortunes in the South. He was a generous philanthropist as well, and his donations were frequently anonymous.

The legacy of Ginter's Gilded Age generation sprang forth in his niece, Grace Arents. As one of the recipients of his estate, Grace continued Lewis Ginter's mission for a better Richmond. She epitomized both the women's movement of the time as well as the wealthy push to philanthropy. There was a concentrated population of Welsh immigrants living in the Oregon Hill neighborhood of Richmond. Most of these people labored in the ironworks and factories. Conditions were meager at best; housing was without running water, and minor children worked in the factories without receiving an education. Grace Arents had her pulse on reform, and she had the resources and innovative nature to back it up. She started the first free public library in Richmond. Richmond public baths, another Grace Arents project, brought low-cost bathing facilities to the neighborhoods without indoor plumbing. She financed the building of at least three Episcopal churches in Richmond. Grace was an innovator in education as well, embracing the social reform of The Settlement House Movement. Its goal was to bring the rich and the poor of society together in physical proximity and social interconnectedness. Its main objective was to establish "settlement houses" in impoverished urban areas, in which volunteer middle class "settlement workers" would live, hoping to share knowledge and culture with and alleviate the poverty of their low-income neighbors. The settlement houses provided services such as daycare, education, and healthcare to improve the lives of the poor in these areas.

Grace was a trained nurse and established the Richmond chapter of the Instructive Visiting Nurses Association, which provides no-cost Home Health Care to the uninsured. Grace pushed for reform in child labor laws, established, and funded the tuition-free private school, St. Andrews, to help educate the neighborhood children and include a night school for working children and adults. St. Andrews School is still active today and maintains Grace Arents' original mission.

Against the rising tide of racism, the modern black community was changing. The Progressive Era was the first generation post-slavery. Maggie Walker was another prominent Richmond native whose mother had been a slave and father a Confederate soldier. Maggie Walker began her formative years caring for the sick and elderly with the Order of St. Luke, an organization she served with until she died. She was also the first African American woman to charter a bank in the United States and served as chairperson of the board after the bank merged with two other large Richmond banks. Like Grace Arents, Maggie Walker was very involved in public education. One of her legacies is the prestigious Maggie Walker Governor's School in Richmond, Virginia.

The Progressive Era took American life from the early cries of free-dom to a country with a quality of life that attracted people from all over the world to the American Ideal. This juncture in history witnessed a shift in American patriotism. We took freedoms, individuality, and equality to a new level. Because of those freedoms and the belief in the individual, capitalism was born in America—American know-how. The freedom to create your own destiny: capitalism created jobs, industrial innovation, the emergence of managerial operations, and the American middle class. This prosperity invited free thought, philoso-phy, and the continued determination to improve life and live those freedoms. Women broke out of traditional roles. The ideas that would benefit society in terms of education, health, and welfare were prom-inent. Philanthropy became a solid indicator of the super wealthy's ability to demonstrate their commitment to improving society for the greater good.

By the turn of the 20th century, the United States was officially a superpower. We had abandoned isolationism—born of the desire for freedom from tyranny that matured into a developed nation of substan-tial economic, military, technological, and cultural strength. Americans found themselves in the enviable position of being global *influencers*. Reminding us of the adage, *"be careful what you wish for,"* as the United States was now front and center on the world's stage.

CHAPTER 7

How History Has Shaped and Destroyed Civilizations

Is exceptionalism part of our patrimony, and does it define American Patriotism? Find a country on this planet that is passionate about their patriotism and all that defines it, and you will find that they consider themselves exceptional. It is often what makes any country remarkable. However, exceptionalism obscures a society's vision when a nation is not willing to look in the mirror. So many elements of great civilizations like ancient Greece and Rome are employed in our modern culture. Our democracy, style of government, the Olympic Games, and sewage and water collection are patterned after innovations by societies that existed 3,000 years ago. These societies were generators. Their population was abundant with a diversity of doers and creators. These great societies are gone, but live on in different iterations worldwide, and are very much a part of the American culture.

What destroys a great civilization? The very *human* nature of the power struggle predestines the human race to repeat history throughout time.

Ode to a Grecian Urn

Ancient Greece was a powerful and glorious civilization full of great thinkers, passionate storytellers, and strategic warriors. They valued physical strength and athleticism, creating the Olympic Games over 2,700 years ago. Their lasting achievements are significant: they took what they had at their disposal and created a society of producers. Great thinkers and philosophers such as Plato, Socrates, Epictetus, and Aristotle are still cited almost 3,000 years later and are the basis for modern philosophic thought. They understood the human condition and human nature. For all of the change we have gone through over the millennia, the human condition is one thing that remains the same. The works of timeless storytellers Aesop and Homer are still taught to our youth through <u>Aesop's Fables</u>, <u>The Iliad</u>, and <u>The Odyssey</u>.

The Greeks were great inventors: the water mill expedited manufacturing. The odometer created a measurement of the distance across their vast lands. The alarm clock, amazingly enough, was a rudimentary Greek invention. The basis of geometry, which was further defined as needing rules for deductive reasoning, was fathered by Miletus, and Pythagoras contributed the Pythagorean Theorem.

Master artisans created beautiful works of treasured antiquity, Grecian Urns. These urns were functional vessels of everyday use to store food, water, and wine. They were beautifully decorated and meticulously crafted with materials that have stood the test of time to give us a glimpse of Grecian life. They incorporated geometry in the trimming with Greek Keys, and they told stories of great battles and heroic people. Keats wrote a powerful poem thousands of years later romanticizing the great civilization, leaving the reader with the question: what happened to this prolific civilization of generators of art and philosophy, science and mathematics, medicine and engineering, athleticism and skilled warriors?

We know from history that there was considerable conflict and competition between city-states in Greece, and it fractured the community within Greece as a whole. War increased tension and conflict. Alliances were shifting, and the war was costly for their society. There was mounting tension and conflict between the ruling class and those at a disadvantage. Does any of this sound familiar? It should. Human nature and power struggle remain consistent within the greatest of societies throughout recorded time.

Rome Was Not Built in a Day

What happened to Greece? Rome. Unstable countries provide the greatest opportunities. While tension and conflict swelled within Greece, a growing Roman Empire took full advantage of Greece's internal turmoil. Rome was significantly larger, more powerful, and their ability to trade throughout the Mediterranean north to the British Isles and south to the northern shores of Africa and Western Asia made them a dominant force. Today the ruins of the Roman Empire have the Greek civilization buried below like layers of lasagna.

Religion played another critical role in the conquering and transitioning of Greek and Roman societies. Both civilizations recognized religions of many Gods, not one God. While the names for each God were different between the Romans and Greeks, their faiths were remarkably similar. It was a transition of the old gods and the new, not a transition of faith.

Rome's contributions to modern society were substantial. Roman architecture became a foundation for Western civilization with the engineering of the Roman Arch and magnificent structures such as the Colosseum and the Pantheon. Their road systems were very sophisticated and still visible today in Rome, along the Appian Way, and Pompeii. They had a system for gutters and developed aqueducts to collect and channel water into villages and cities. The remnants of these innovations are found not just in Rome, but also throughout Roman provinces in France, Spain, the Dalmatian Coastline, Greece, and Ephesus. The Romans laid the framework for the modern legal system and government. As a significant military power, Roman advances were substantial. They innovated in weapons, military strategy, and medical corps on the field of battle.

Like the Grecian Urn, Latin literature has stood the test of time and built on Greece's literature with classic works by authors such as Ovid, Horace, Cicero, and Virgil remaining on reading lists today. The Romans were responsible for the first semblance of a newspaper with the "Acta Diurna" enabling citizens to gather in specified locations throughout Roman cities to read the news or "actions of the day," which were chiseled on stone tablets. Our modern calendar is based on the Julian calendar of Rome. The Roman numeral system is still in use, thousands of years later. These are all products of a society of great generators and doers that still endure. What happened to this grand society?

Greed: The provinces of the empire paid heavy taxes to support the opulence of the City of Rome. Conflict and social unrest resulted from the widening gap between the rich and the poor. Slave labor affected the economy by taking jobs from tradespeople. The Roman Empire grew so large and became so affluent it lost sight of caring for its society as a whole and focused on materialism and lux lifestyle.

Political Unrest: There was conflict and corruption within the government. Overspending on the military and overexpansion not only caused inflation but also stretched the Roman military too far. Through a series of poor military decisions, chinks began to develop in Rome's armor. These weaknesses provided an opportunity. Barbarian Tribes from the north and east watched and waited for their moments. Rome began to crumble and recede as an empire and a civilization.

Christianity: For the first time, there was a growing faith in one God. A massive shift occurred in religious values for an Empirical civilization whose citizenry had favored multiple gods for centuries. It took time, but Christianity took hold in Rome as it eroded traditional Roman values and pagan beliefs in favor of one God. There was no hierarchy in the Christian belief, and with that, the aristocratic entitlements were no longer justifiable. The welfare of ordinary people factored heavily in the spread of Christianity. Rome began to slowly disappear until all that was left were ransacked ruins pillaged for their marble and gold.

A Journey of a Thousand Miles Begins with a Single Step

The ancient Chinese civilization has a more extended history than ancient Greece and Rome and has evolved the most into the modern era. As we experience the global events of the present day, it is incredibly relevant to understand China's history. The Chinese people have a civilization that has disintegrated and reemerged throughout the millennia. They are a global force to be reckoned with while having a history that is older than any world power today. The history of China has been an isolated civilization, but their advancements rivaled those of the more centralized Greek and Roman cultures. The Chinese Dynasties stretch far back in dated artifacts to 2100-1600 BC.

What makes the Chinese Dynastic civilization so remarkable is that it lasted for approximately 4,000 years. For a country thousands of miles and a hemisphere away, China's ancient history has had a substantial impact on our society. They have consistently woven in and out of eras of totalitarian rule, suppression of dissenting thought, and social change while becoming a military superpower and an economic rival.

One of the most impactful people from Chinese history is Confucius, who lived during the tumultuous Zhou Dynasty of the first century BC. His philosophy and teachings have endured throughout millennia. He influenced Chinese thought and culture for many centuries, focusing on family, loyalty, righteousness, and humanity's value. Confucius encouraged *"shu"* (reciprocity): never force on others what you would not choose for yourself. He was not just a moral guide for human character. He described in detail the importance of education, and that reward should be based on merit, not on entitlement. No blue ribbons for participation. He guided political philosophy with what he considered the three most important duties of government: the confidence of the people in their government, food supply in balance with the people's needs, and the military power necessary to protect the people. He promoted self-government, harmony, benevolence, and virtue in society. These teachings have influenced cultures throughout the world over many centuries.

These ancient philosophies are timeless contributions to civilization. However, Confucian thought has been erased from modern-day China. How did this evolve for China? As with most world aristocracies, the dynastic system crumbled—in 1912—and was replaced with a central government. China abandoned Confucianism in an attempt to move toward Western thinking and become a more global society. The importance of the sciences and democracy became a new standard in Chinese culture, and The Culture Movement was born. There was a focus on democratic values, freedoms, and women's liberation. It was a time of prolific Chinese literature and art.

Occupation→Liberation→Subjugation

The Chinese culture experienced a "Roaring Twenties" of its own for many decades. When the Japanese occupation of China occurred during WWII, it became a tipping point for structured change for a post-war China. For a society that had outlasted any of the great civilizations, it was a rude awakening. The move was swift and totalitarian. Mao Zedong's government brought communism to China. Horrific events like the Great Leap Forward of the late 1950s and early 1960s, were designed as a five-year plan to transform China from an agrarian nation to an industrial nation. The focus shifted aggressively to industrial economic power and away from private farming, which became prohibited and was replaced with collective agriculture. Failed innovations resulted in destroyed agriculture, polluted soil, and waterways. Forced labor, torture as punishment for dissent, and extreme subjugation brought on scaled economic and environmental destruction. The results of these events were disastrous and tragic. It was an enormous event of mass killing in human history, and a complete failure in socialism and centralized planning. We tend to forget that the Great Leap Forward produced an intentional famine and starvation so sizable that it eclipses the Holocaust, with a loss of life estimated at upwards of 45 million people.

The Cultural Revolution followed, which took the freedoms from Chinese society that expressed anything capitalistic as well as any long-honored and cherished Chinese traditions. Artists were paraded through the streets in public humiliation, bound in chains with signs around their necks, condemning their artistic expression of traditional Chinese culture as works of a dissenter. They were tortured, imprisoned, and their properties seized. From the 1970s to the present day, there have been attempts at restoring democracy in China to no avail, resulting in massacres within Chinese territories, Tiananmen Square, and the present-day Hong Kong Protests.

China has become a world superpower with a commitment to communism. They are now the only world power with that distinction. The level of Chinese trade with the rest of the world is outer-stratosphere, as evidenced by the most recent events of COVID-19, as companies worldwide scrambled to have empty shipping pallets and containers return from the ports in China, to facilitate the distribution of consumer staples globally.

According to the 2018 Juwai Chinese Global Property Investment Report, Chinese real estate investments internationally have risen from five billion to 120 billion dollars in seven years. Their most extensive real estate holdings are in the United States, Hong Kong, the United Kingdom, and Australia—all English-speaking and democracies.

The Chinese population has millions of people living in poverty. It is the "People's Republic of China." Their brand of communism is propped up with human rights violations and sweatshop labor. China has fueled its ability to trade globally and compete with lower prices through slavery under the guise of "the people's war on terror." With the banner of thwarting extremism headlining their cause, they have created internment camps—"re-education camps" for Muslims, Christians, and other ethnic minority groups within China. The numbers are estimated in the hundreds of thousands, perhaps a million. This internment camp population provides free labor to manufacture tremendous amounts of lower-priced products that the rest of the world buys from China.

Why is this Important?

Cautionary tales, historical perspective, and human nature all come into play when analyzing what makes an exemplary society and what can take it down. Strip away politics, religion, and cultural differences—we are all human beings. There are always going to be aggressors, reactors, instigators as well as generators. The question is how do human beings move society forward?

A state of mindfulness and perspective in anything we do as humans is our first line of defense in understanding how to create a society that propels us forward. So that the teachings of the great philosophers like Confucius are not lost, it is critical to remember, digest, and understand not just history but also the present day. We play out the power struggle game throughout centuries of significant advancements. Our societies are more affluent, more global, with rapidly changing technological and scientific progress. What makes our modern culture and civilization so different from the ancient civilizations that did not survive?

Power struggle is the Achilles Heel of the human race. There is a tremendous void in benevolence and harmony. Patriotism, as faith in the country and each other, does not come without the determination to work together to realize a common purpose and achieve common goals. To grant benevolence to those with whom we interact, even when we disagree, is to exercise character and virtue even when our agendas contain special interests that do not achieve a balance.

CHAPTER 8

Change is Constant and History Repeats

Our country as a nation is less than 250 years old. Our ancestors were in Jamestown in 1607, but America was not born as a nation until 1776. We colonized a new world, adjusted to an untamed land, attempted to survive famine, disease, and some of the challenges we brought on ourselves, "coexisting," or not, with Native Americans. Our European counterparts were living in 17th-century prosperity—the Baroque period—famously excessive and ornate. It was a time of the Golden Age for most of Western Europe. It was a time of great scientific and mathematical discovery abroad.

In comparison, the American Gilded Age would not happen for another 200+ years. The first Americans, in 1607 Jamestown, were mostly living as medieval Europeans in the 1500s. Why does this matter? Because there is a cadence to the evolution of any society as it prospers: that *change* is constant, history does repeat itself, and humans are predisposed to certain behaviors throughout history. Current events are happening that may appear to have a new face, but the circumstances are those that evolve from historical repeats. It is vital to be watchful and mindful of this.

The first decade of the 20th century ushered in Teddy Roosevelt as a major reformer. He enacted anti-trust and anti-monopoly laws to increase competition in the workplace and created jobs and innovations that stabilized the economy and created a fairer marketplace. He established the Food and Drug Administration to protect the American food supply, and he created the National Park System to preserve and conserve our natural treasures. Roosevelt championed a pro-American vision while understanding where our evolving American society took its place globally. He saw international trade and security as significant issues for a country that had grown immeasurably through the tenets of democracy and capitalism.

Roosevelt's foreign policy actions may have set the U.S. up for involvement in WWI, or they may have been the brilliantly calculated foresight of a man who saw the inherent risks of building a great nation. He built the Panama Canal to increase ease of trade—and for security. He committed to a long-term presence in the Philippines, along with an expanded American Navy. He resurrected the Monroe Doctrine to ensure Congress and the world knew that intervention by external influences in the Americas' politics was a potentially hostile act against the United States. As Roosevelt dramatically increased the size of American Naval forces, he then just as dramatically paraded American fleets around the world.

Domestically, Teddy Roosevelt was on both the side of business and labor. Internationally, he held similar beliefs in the balance of power and the inception of international agencies to protect that balance. Teddy Roosevelt was not a great orator with the gift of verbally pacifying the nation with words of reassurance. His talents manifested through measurable actions. He understood the need to rebuild trust within our American society.

An Intercepted Telegram, Sinking Ships and a War to End All Wars

At the Second Virginia Convention in 1775, after vigorous debate and an impassioned, well-articulated speech by Patrick Henry, Americans decided that a war was necessary. As the U.S. entered World War I, familiar circumstances emerged as well. The United States had resolved to stay neutral for over two years concerning the war in Europe. Less than 150 years earlier, American colonists had the same concerns about a war with Great Britain.

The United States of the early 1900s was undoubtedly a model of not only capitalistic prosperity and industrial prowess but also world-renown in advances in medicine, science, and education. We had social reforms to include an emerging middle class. As Americans enjoyed a desirable quality of life, disturbing reports were coming from Germany about its aggressor status in Europe. There was tremendous political upheaval in Russia, a country with a much greater landmass than the United States. We had our ears to the ground. No one wants what war inevitably brings: loss of life and financial deficit. The decision to go to war weighs heavily against the cost to society. Woodrow Wilson went to Congress in 1917, in a scene not unlike Patrick Henry's argument for war in 1775. Woodrow Wilson saw this entry into the war, with the Allies against Germany as a "war to end all wars." Patrick Henry similarly pointed out that Great Britain had armies and navies positioned all around the colonial borders, with no apparent enemies, while the Colonies lay defenseless and weak.

> *We have petitioned; we have remonstrated; we have suppli-*
> *cated; we have prostrated ourselves before the throne, and*
> *have implored its interposition to arrest the tyrannical*
> *hands of the ministry and Parliament. Our petitions have*
> *been slighted; our remonstrances have produced additional*
> *violence and insult; our supplications have been disregarded;*
> *and we have been spurned, with contempt, from the foot of*
> *the throne.* — Excerpt from Patrick Henry's speech to the
> Virginia Convention 1775

In the instance of WWI, the sinking of the RMS Lusitania was not the only catalyst for the U.S. entering the war. Torpedoing a British passenger ship and killing 1,200 people on board as retaliation for a naval blockade provided a clear picture of the degree of aggression Germany was willing to employ to achieve its goals. For the U.S., the defining moment came with the Zimmermann Telegram, a communication intercepted by the British. Germany extended an offer to Mexico to regain territory lost during the Mexican-American War. While U.S. officials were absorbing this intercepted information, German U-boats began sinking American merchant ships in the North Atlantic.

While change during 100 years had brought the U.S. to superpower status, it did not prevent the symmetry of historical repetition. In 1917, with our merchant ships torpedoed in the Atlantic and clandestine alliances forming between our bordering neighbors and a totalitarian government, we were revisiting 1812 when Great Britain sank our merchant ships in the Atlantic and attempted to form secret alliances with Native Americans.

These historical repeats rely not just on circumstance but also on human nature; one is the eternal struggle for power and dominance, and the other, revolt against tyranny and inhumanity. Historical change and events move through great societies that not only populated ancient lands with great cities but also created and inspired great thinkers in science, philosophy, athletics, and the arts; cultures that celebrated the individual. Great societies that celebrate the individual encourage great producers. Independence may have been born as an American ideal, but it took courage to imagine it and bravery to execute the steps necessary to achieve independence. Power struggles have the inherent potential to threaten the individual, progress, and society. For this reason alone, as we move through societal change, we will also inevitably repeat history.

Unstable Countries are the Greatest of Opportunities

World War I changed everything for the United States. Before the Great War, we were a country working on expansionism within our territories and building an industrial empire. We were changing how women were viewed in society. After several years of neutrality, the U.S. entered a war that was not fought on our soil, and not one that we initiated. World War I became a global crisis, and American involvement in this war forever changed our commitment at home and abroad. Men shipped out to fight in battles overseas as women replaced them in factories, working to keep American commerce moving. We entered the war to remove Germany's threat to the U.S. and preserve democracy around the world. We ended the war with a vision, much like American expansionism, which became a blueprint for new world order.

There is always a cost—our American patriotism shifted again—we were now the protector of democracy around the world. Woodrow Wilson's League of Nations created alliances with European countries to ensure security throughout the international community and remove the threat of aggression. For many Americans, this post-war world carried bitterness and unrest over concerns that neglecting an "America First" mentality, allowed us to lose our focus to continue to improve American society. Congress never ratified U.S. membership in the League for that very reason—as many felt the U.S. needed to return to the era of American isolationism. Despite our reluctance and rejection of the League's ratification, the U.S. still emerged from WWI, a military superpower and defender of freedom internationally. The League of Nations dissolved with no congressional buy-in. The U.S. was out; there was no eagerness on the part of European nations to continue the League. The U.S. had become integral in peacekeeping, military force, and financial backing. The "war to end all wars" would not be the last. The financial bailouts for war-ravaged countries would become a recurring circumstance for the U.S. American protest over U.S. involvement in WWI would occur again with Vietnam and continued with the Middle East.

A Decade Long Happy Hour Led to a Crippling Hangover

There was nothing Americans wanted more post-WWI than to focus on American life. We shifted back to an insular society. American women were more empowered to leave domestic life and earn a living outside the home. During the war years, when men left their jobs to become soldiers, women filled their vacancies. Women became nurses to care for the sick and wounded. The Suffragettes took on journalism and literary circles.

For the first time in our country's history, the population in urban environments eclipsed those living in rural areas. Big business and industry grew as the American economy doubled during the 1920s. Corporations essentially established the growth of middle management and the middle class. A consumer-driven society was unfamiliar to the average American. What changed was the "Average Joe" was making money—and he was spending it. The exploding automobile industry gave anyone with a job paying enough the ability to afford a car, freedom on the open road. The car represented one of the first middle-class status symbols. A family who owned a vehicle had achieved financial success.

Cities provided the means to earn a higher income in burgeoning American enterprise, and cities provided the environment to spend that increased income, as entertainment became an alluring draw. People wanted to forget the drab war years of hardship and sacrifice to reward themselves with a lifestyle that cost more than they earned. It was the age of jazz clubs, art, and literary societies that invited men and women as equals. However, not everyone was dancing the Charleston. Farmers and coal miners suffered tremendously during this time. Electricity challenged supply and demand for the coal industry as the new energy source forced many mines to shut down. Farmers were tasked with a vast population to feed—a favorable problem, in terms of demand. However, they could not keep up with the rising cost of equipment (that would ultimately increase their productivity), and against the lower crop prices, farmers were getting squeezed. These innovations brought a significant change of circumstance for a country that not more than 50 years prior had been a mostly agricultural economy.

Layered over, all of this was an international political time bomb. Europe expected financial reparations from Germany to rebuild their cities after the war. The U.S. expected to be reimbursed by Europe for coming to their aid in World War I, and the U.S. had lent Germany the money to make good on those reparations to the rest of Europe. It was a global shell game. World War I and the reparations detailed in the Peace Treaty made the most sizable Western economies too dependent on each other. When banks failed, economies tumbled. The American economy, which was propping up other European countries, teetered and fell as well.

There were no jobs and so there was no income. There was no extension of credit. People lost their homes and packed families in cars to wander from town to town across the country to find day labor. Shantytowns and Hoovervilles popped up with temporary housing, not unlike the refugee camps we witness today in the Middle East via international news outlets. Parents had to make heart-wrenchingly difficult decisions to place their children in orphanages, hoping it would be a temporary measure. They were no longer able to afford to care for their families. Patriotism was at an all-time low—Americans were just trying to survive. The Great Depression resulted in anger, bitterness, despair, and a lack of trust in government.

There is consistent debate, and division, in our nation today over whether we should continue to be the world's influencers for democracy and freedom, and how that impacts America's ability to put "America First." World War I has had far more influence on American life and patriotism today than most realize. Our American ancestors lived in a world that fought for an independent country, with individual freedoms. With independence achieved, they worked to create a society that could build on those freedoms. America lived as a country geographically removed from Western Europe, with only two bordering countries providing a sense of isolationism. We still opened our doors to immigrants willing to work and create their prosperity.

The brilliance of our Founding Fathers is the framework they enacted to accommodate change. That is irrefutably American, change is constant, and Americans became change-makers throughout our 130 + year history before WWI. Our patriotism defended freedoms, and the war elevated an American nationalism abroad as we expanded protectionism beyond American borders. A significant part of what defines American patriotism has been honed over the century since WWI, as the world's watchdog. It came at a price. WWI changed American society at home and our role abroad forever. WWI created American pride and resolve in the face of a foreign threat and taught the U.S. a powerful lesson. When it came to achieving power and status, we were unprepared for what would ensue. We had limited historical context to understand the magnitude of what the Peace Treaty ultimately meant in terms of financial and military obligation.

The Cadence Change That Sounds Strangely Familiar

America in the 1930s was struggling. We were a nation tragically unprepared for the global responsibility we had taken on in WWI. Our financial system crumbled under the strain of both international lending and extending credit at home. The flaws in our banking system were revealed as unregulated and uninsured banks went under, leaving millions of Americans suddenly penniless. The stock market crash was so devastating that some experts estimate that it took several decades for the markets to recover their previous high.

Roughly 25% of the working population was now unemployed. Average Americans were faced with the realities of severe daily financial hardship. Additionally, natural disasters in the Mid-West Plains created the worst drought in American history with colossal dust storms that carried away soil, making agriculture impossible. The dust storms forced a mass evacuation between 1930 and 1940 as over 3.5 million farmers left the Plains States, many moving west to California to start life over.

We hit an all-time low in terms of morale during this time. Patriotism was reduced to a hunkering shadow in the corner. Americans were focused on survival and desperate for leadership change; we elected Franklin D. Roosevelt, who literally "waged war against the (American) emergency." Roosevelt energized American society by enacting more laws to impact the most immediate issues within his first 100 days than what had been accomplished in the previous four years by his predecessor, Herbert Hoover.

Laws were enacted to help farmers, separate commercial and investment banking, and create the Federal Deposit Insurance Corporation (FDIC) to protect depositors. Homeowners were protected from losing their homes with new refinancing terms, and laws protecting fair wages and pricing to stimulate the economy were put into effect. In 1935, Americans were no longer on their knees, but we were still convalescing. FDR came in with the second round of his New Deal, a colossal change-maker for the American economy and the American spirit. The Works Progress Administration meant building societal infrastructure, and it meant jobs. Pure and simple: jobs were created, people went back to work, and the economy started to make strides to improve.

Americans may not realize how many of those 100,000 + projects that employed millions of people are still part of the American landscape. The WPA projects are as much a part of our national heritage, as the Freedom Bell, Old Glory, and the Declaration of Independence. These projects defined the resurrection of American patriotism of the 1930s. They represented pride in engineering infrastructures like the Hoover Dam, the Lincoln Tunnel, and the Overseas Highway linking Miami to Key West. They represented innovations in construction, such as the Chrysler Building and the Empire State Building. They represented the commitment to preserve nature with the Great Smoky Mountain National Park and Camp David.

America's great pastime, baseball's Doubleday Field in Cooperstown, NY, was a WPA product. The arts were not excluded—this was America's moment to employ and generate great works of art in public spaces, such as Coit Tower and Rockefeller Center with the Public Works of Art Project. The Federal Writers Project allowed struggling writers to become paid employees and to write the American Guide Series, which provided city visitors with helpful information. The WPA recognized the need for the diversity of talent in an exceptional society and encouraged and revered progress, perseverance, and resilience.

What happened between 1933 and 1941 uplifted Americans economically and brought us together as a society with the grit and determination that created better lives, renewed faith in our country, and, most importantly, camaraderie—a shared mission. Patriotism and faith in country and each other does not come without commitment to working together to realize a common purpose and set a course to achieve common goals. The historical significance of where we were as a country in terms of economy, pride, patriotism, and working together was vital in preparing the nation for what happened next. December 7, 1941, changed everything. We were poised for yet another historical repeat that decidedly set a course through history and America's role in geopolitics.

"Remember Pearl Harbor..."

... the phrase that has given a warning, for almost 80 years, never to forget. Pearl Harbor symbolizes the U.S. entry into WWII with agreement from Congress. The government declared war on Japan the day following the Pearl Harbor attack. Pearl Harbor should never lose its impact or relevance, as the events leading up to the attack in Hawaii were clear signals of aggression and oppression. Events show the U.S. and Japan were moving in the direction of war for a lengthy period. Japan was very aggressive in its annexation of other countries and territories. The U.S. was extremely concerned about how Japan chose to solve its economic and geographic deficits by taking over China to achieve a mainland presence.

Japan declared war on China in 1937, and the U. S. responded to this hostile act with economic sanctions and trade embargoes. Four years later, Japan's fateful decision to bomb Pearl Harbor initiated a declaration of war from the United States. We lost 2,403 people that morning. Our navy suffered damages to 20 ships and lost the USS Arizona and USS Utah. Three hundred planes were destroyed.

Our country was just getting back on its feet after barely surviving the 1929 Stock Market Crash and the Great Depression. With infinite resiliency and pride in the nation, Americans rose and met the known challenges that war brings to a country and its society. These Americans became known as The Greatest Generation defined by, and survived through WWI, the Great Depression and WWII. To imagine going back to that could be completely demoralizing, but instead, an amazing resolve rooted Americans around the country. Human lives were lost. They became galvanized. We realized that Japan was at our doorstep, and their history was aggressive and threatened democracy. Germany attacked countries throughout Europe for a solid two years before the U.S. entered WWII in 1941, for the same reasons as the Japanese aggressions. Germany's acts threatened democracy and human rights around the world. This short history should sound familiar, not just because it revives textbook memories in the classroom but also because we regularly revisit the past. The circumstances are different, as the world changes over time. Still, we continue to repeat history time and again. The ledger of modern history records page after page in economic sanctions and trade embargoes as the firm stance we take when fair trade, human rights, atrocities, weapons build-up, breach of the law, treaty, or Act have been compromised. It is the first warning line drawn and has been since the American Revolution.

My generation has known economic sanctions with the Middle East almost our entire lives. We lived a Cold War existence with Russia for decades, which now extends to China. This geopolitical cause and effect feel palatable compared to engaged conflict and warfare: Korea and Vietnam marked the first of a succession of failed involvements abroad that redirected our focus from what we were doing wrong in our backyard.

9/11 was America's 21st century Pearl Harbor. No one could imagine the horrific magnitude of what happened once again on American soil. It was unfathomable to conceive of the way the attack was perpetrated. Terrorism's subversive evil shook Americans to the core. Two thousand nine hundred and seventy-seven innocent victims of terrorism died that day, and another 6,000 people were injured. We were utterly unprepared as a nation watching terror happen on live television, and it forever changed American vigilance in daily life. 9/11 was a deliberate act of aggression that propelled the U.S. to invade Afghanistan and remove al-Qaeda. Two years later, we justified an invasion of Iraq to remove Saddam Hussein from power along with the order to destroy weapons of mass destruction that were never discovered.

Americans have become indifferent to conflict post-Vietnam. The Iraq War lasted for seven years, and in 2014, after the war had subsided for three years, we re-engaged in conflict with Iraq. Several generations of Americans overlap with differing generational perspectives, but the overarching feeling among most is reluctant support compared to the World War era. We have become desensitized by the 24-hour broadcast news cycle. Rather than focus our efforts on making our own country a better place, we allowed fear to affect who we interacted with.

A new era emerged of renewed American Patriotism trying to grab hold of the life preserver of homeland security. There is no doubt the U.S. needed to shore up the chinks in the homeland armor. We did so at the expense of intense racial biases, profiling, and distrust—the same historical practice with a new face. This era, spanning Korea, Vietnam, Cuba, Desert Storm, Iran, and our involvement in South American countries, were circumstances where Americans seemed to learn little from history. We adopted ourselves as the world's police, and we allowed ego and power to reign rather than historical insight and reason.

What the Great American Novel and 2,000 Year Old Tomes Tell Us about History and Human Nature

Add resolute intention to freedom and equality, and it is amazing what human beings can visualize and create when given the freedom to do so. The possibilities are infinite. Historical repeats happen for many reasons, the circumstances are ever changing and the human condition—how human beings engage in those circumstances throughout history becomes a tale often told.

Literature confirms throughout recorded time that if there is one element that does not change, it is human nature. We have read 2,000-year-old books that chronicle the stories and parables of human behavior. The Bible and the Qu'ran maintain some relevance as religious stories for the faithful and as parables illustrating the good and evil in human nature. The ancient Chinese Taoist tome, The Art of War, has had a similar effect. The book has been used for centuries after its original discovery for its brilliance in military strategy but has also found purpose in corporate business, law, and sports. These books of antiquity may not directly portray American life, but have a place at the core of our American patriotism, modeling the drive to find purpose and do better.

Influential American literary classics such as The Great Gatsby, The Grapes of Wrath, or To Kill a Mockingbird, each portrays periods in American history that reflect American society's evolution. They chronicle the lives of Americans during the Gilded Age, the Great Depression, and the Civil Rights Era and give real faces to humanity's struggles. They are the cautionary tales, told fictionally, about humanity in the face of adversity and greed, hunger and excess, inequality, and injustice.

Ironically, these books have come to define America in ways that *Common Sense*, The Declaration of Independence, and The U.S. Constitution cannot. Events in a timeline and the framework for a society governed by its people are a monochrome of black and white, while the American novel gives color to humanity. They depict circumstance, cause and effect, and broader questions about who we want to be as human beings, our struggles, our frailties, and our successes. They represent the beauty and the heritage of American life in all of its triumphs and failures. We are fascinated by stories that depict life fictionally but describe the "every man." Sometimes these are the novels that strike at the heart of controversy and philosophy and incite the reader to develop their credo based on characters that embody traits or philosophies that reflect integrity, insight, and benevolence. Novels like Ayn Rand's <u>Atlas Shrugged</u> and Tom Wolfe's <u>Bonfire of the Vanities</u> are works that confront individual and societal morality and then address the human traits that deliver the best and the worst to society within the confines of historical fiction.

Historical context should resonate when it is examined with a reasoning eye for circumstantial evidence. What are the facts? What was the cause, and ultimately, what was the effect? What historical fiction lends to history are the rich details that expose societal implications. It digs deep into the human psyche of that moment in time. Literature can explore human nature, and it exposes power and corruption. It celebrates the triumph of the human spirit.

In an excerpt from the August 28, 2014 issue of *The New Yorker*, Adam Gopnik writes:

> *"The real sin that the absence of a historical sense encourages is presentism, in the sense of exaggerating our present problems out of all proportion to those that have previously existed. It lies in believing that things are much worse than they have ever been—and, thus, than they really are—or are uniquely threatening rather than familiarly difficult."*

Adam Gopnik's statement is an excellent reminder for us all that we need to *remember history*. When we make that reconnection to historical events, we recognize that the problems we are currently encountering are strangely familiar to the circumstances and troubles of the past. The great successes of world leaders were realized because they studied historical perspective very carefully. They followed sequences of events and political and economic climates to understand better why a particular course of action occurred. Then they looked at where society was at that time and what choices were available. Our most significant failures are when we turn a blind eye to the naked truth, buy into the justifications of story, and fail to act with reason in a direction—a solution that moves society forward.

There will always be great thinkers and doers who are generators, propelling society forward throughout time. There will always be people in history who prey on a broken nation, who can engage the hopeless through sociopathic charisma devoid of character. It is the cycle of history entangled with humanity. One of the most beautiful, and arguably the most enviable hallmarks of our American patrimony—our heritage—our patriotism—is that we strive to improve. As human beings, one of our greatest challenges is that we get in our own way. We create self-imposed obstacles with free-will and power struggle, as we try to get better at what we do.

CHAPTER 9

How has Patriotism Changed in America?

The decades after WWII and the new millennium brought lightning speed change for the nation and a new fluidity to American society and patriotism. Eras were no longer necessarily defined by decades. Technology accelerates time. Lifestyle and workplace efficiencies happened at such a rapid pace, changing our culture to the extent that embracing constant change has *become* the new culture.

Think about the enormity of this: The U.S.—and most first and second world countries—have experienced explosive growth over the last 75 years. This growth and change used to take centuries to achieve. The end of WWII brought Americans home to focus on American life. Rather than the return home from the Great War to revelry that ultimately led to financial disaster, Americans got to work to ensure that the freedoms we fought for abroad continued to be preserved and elevated at home.

The Rise of Second World Countries

The Soviet Union's strength and alliance during WWII was one of the tipping points in winning the war over Germany. Post-WWII, no one wanted a repeat of the burden the financial bailouts and war debts of post-WWI placed on Germany, the rest of Western Europe and the U.S. The world was still reeling from the Nazi's atrocities against Jews and other minorities. Not only were Americans and the Allied countries of WWII focused on improving the lives of their respective citizens, but the international spotlight was on bringing war criminals to justice for the horrors of the Holocaust.

The aftermath of WWII brought the Soviet Union into prominence as one of the two greatest military superpowers of their time. As mentioned in the previous chapter, unstable countries are the greatest of opportunities. The Soviet Union took the Eastern half of Germany, with Berlin split at its center, and continued to systematically annex all of Eastern Europe. Communist regimes between the Soviet Union, its annexed countries and China achieved the level of occupying one third of the world's land mass. For the U.S. and the Soviet Union, the Cold War was a time of distrust between both nations. Here were two superpowers with totally different societal systems—Capitalistic Democracy vs. Totalitarian Communism—and ironically, two nations with a very strong and similar patriotism. Imagine the mounting distrust that builds between nations confronted by an alter ego. The Soviet Union could match power and force with the U.S. militarily, and with the space race and the nuclear arms race.

The growing threat was revealed in totalitarian expansionism, the U.S.S.R. was amassing great populations with strategic geography. Affluent America was thriving during this time in a democracy; the U.S.S.R. was growing in strength and power in military and government, but did not have the quality of life enjoyed by Americans. U.S. patriotism re-identified American faith in the freedoms of democracy with the quality of life free markets provided. Communism had become the fear for Modern Era Americans, just as sovereignty had been to Colonial Americans.

On the Wings of Victory

Facilitation, efficiency and productivity drove this era of American prosperity. The GI Bill provided the nation with a well-educated work force. Infrastructure was improved and expanded with the Interstate Highway System changing how quickly and efficiently Americans could move around the country by car. Trucking competed with the railroads to deliver goods to more remote areas without the constraints of a freight train timetable. Distribution warehouses populated the country facilitating the movement of goods and increasing supply to meet demand. Oil costs were low, which was not only beneficial to businesses, but also allowed Americans the choice to live in suburbs and drive into the city for work. Post-WWII was the beginning of suburban sprawl: the American dream of home ownership, the white picket fence and two cars in the driveway. Manufacturing, transportation and technology drove the U.S. economy along with the automobile industry, aviation and television and computer technology. Labor unions became very prominent in protecting the middle-class American worker. The economy and the middle class grew exponentially.

Simultaneously, American agriculture was changing. New chemical technologies brought pesticides and fertilizers to farmers to protect crops. Massive combine harvesters efficiently brought the food supply to market in record time. In turn, farmers were able to replant their crops quickly to repeat the growth cycle and provide for growing demand.

The American population post-war was lower. Remember, too, that prior to WWII the U.S. had been recovering from the Great Depression. Americans during the Depression era were not having larger families and sometimes had to make the difficult decision to place the children they did have in orphanages. That was not the case post-1945: renewed optimism in the economy and the country encouraged a soaring birth rate. Americans born from 1945 until 1964 would become the Baby Boomer generation and the largest generation in history, at that time. This generation had the greatest influence on American culture for 50 years. A new American culture was developing around the golden age of capitalism and a new affluence amongst the middle class. The most compelling numbers of the era spoke to the tremendous economic growth happening during the 15-year period between 1945 and 1960. As told by William H. Chafe in The Unfinished Journey: America Since World War II:

GNP grew by 250%.

- New construction expense multiplied nine times.

- Personal consumption services increased three times.

- 1960 saw per capita income 35% higher than in 1945.

- Short-term credit went up from $8.4 billion in 1946 to $45.6 billion in 1958.

As a result of the postwar economic boom, 60% of the American population had attained a 'middle-class' standard of living by the mid-50s (defined as incomes of $3,000 to $10,000 in constant dollars), compared with only 31% in the last year of prosperity before the onset of the Great Depression. By the end of the decade, 87% of families owned a TV set, 75% a car, and 75% a washing machine.

American life was good. The population that served in WWII was still alive and actively employed. This generation of war veterans was not only improving the quality of life Americans were enjoying, but they were also a proud reminder of those who served this great country and who had been victorious in WWII. They were a clear representation of American patriotism both at home and abroad—both economically and as protectors of freedom.

The Importance of Détente

The Cold War is very important to understand with regard to how we and other nations deal with conflict and diplomacy. After two World Wars and 37 million military and civilian casualties, the global détente became a strong commitment from the 1950s to the late 1980s. This was the first time in history that war had the potential to be waged through long range missiles, rather than by soldiers fighting on land or sea. Long range missiles are tools of aggression that can do maximum damage with little to no human involvement, or loss of life. However, this type of warfare also brought the grim reality that any city or town could be targeted and destroyed by a nervous trigger finger. The ability to ease tensions through diplomatic communication was paramount to ensuring the Soviet Union and the U.S. approached their differences with a level of resolve and decorum. Whether countries fundamentally disagree on almost any issue, détente symbolized the ability to respectfully disagree and continue to work toward mutually agreed upon terms solving mutual problems.

The Cold War signaled for Americans that although apprehension (the Cuban Missile Crisis) and distrust (Cold War espionage) lingered in the air, we were able to move forward to improve the nation, while maintaining a determined effort to mitigate international tensions without declaring war.

A Turning Tide and Faded Glory

Capitalist expansionism allowed middle class Americans to achieve a quality of life by 1963 that was approaching the twenty-year mark. Twenty years of prosperity and growth created a consumption climate. Technology and convenience changed life dramatically during this time. Advertising and marketing companies became as profitable as the businesses they were promoting. American patriotism has always represented freedoms. Just as importantly, our patriotism has represented individual freedoms that allow society to always move forward with the goal of continued improvement. In 1960, we had just elected the youngest president in the history of our country and Americans were energized by his enthusiasm for the country, his passion for renewing patriotism and his commitment to change.

John F. Kennedy's relatability encouraged a younger generation of Americans to accept the responsibility that comes with the American Dream: the call to each and every one of us to make a difference. He inspired a generation of social change and mindful vigilance abroad. Excerpts from his 1960 nomination acceptance speech speak to an identified American complacency, and the importance of looking forward and moving forward toward change:

> ... the New Frontier is here, whether we seek it or not. Beyond that frontier are the uncharted areas of science and space, unsolved problems of peace and war, unconquered pockets of ignorance and prejudice, unanswered questions of poverty and surplus ... courage—not complacency—is our need today—leadership—not salesmanship.... Must we sacrifice our future in order to enjoy the present? That is the question of the New Frontier. That is the choice our nation must make ...between national greatness and national decline—between the fresh air of progress and the stale, dank atmosphere of "normalcy"—between determined dedication and creeping mediocrity. All mankind waits upon our decision. A whole world looks to see what we will do. We cannot fail their trust, we cannot fail to try.

This was a movement of social change faced with the threat of growing Communist influence globally and it woke Americans up.

American society was ready for strong patriotic direction in the face of the Communist threat in Russia, and the imminent fear the Cuban Missile Crisis cast over the entire country. School children did bomb shelter drills daily in school. To give perspective on the degree of vigilance Americans took to everyday life: I was born in 1964, and we were still doing these drills in the early 1970s. Safety drills were a reengagement in the mentality that took hold of Americans after Pearl Harbor—the visceral reality that acts of aggression could happen on American soil.

America's Great Shame

Slavery ended in 1865 and we still were not making it right a century later, but the 1960s brought promise and hope. Civil Rights are a global issue and not just unique to Americans. However, we are the world's change-makers and the rest of the world has watched our struggle unfold on American soil for a century and a half. The history of Civil Rights in America repeats with small steps of resolution over a very long history. We fought a homeland war over slavery. By 1865, slavery was abolished, but were Americans moving in the direction of equality?

The Jim Crow Laws—State and local laws enacted by Democratic-led southern states during the 1870s Reconstruction Era—epitomized blatant discrimination. These laws represented "States' rights" advocated and enforced by the Southern United States, which legalized racial segregation until 1965. The Jim Crow Laws were the inability of the South to let go of the practice of slavery by stripping African Americans of their constitutional rights via laws and tests.

The Southern states had laws of segregation for almost 100 years after the Civil War. The rest of the country does not get a free pass on this issue. Even without the presence of segregation laws in the rest of the country, segregation was practiced in almost every environment. The 1960s took the Civil Rights Movement to a place of prominence on the television screen. Every television-owning American, no matter if you lived in Idaho, New York, Kansas or Mississippi, witnessed unwavering bravery and commitment to equality in American heroes like Martin Luther King, Jr., Rosa Parks and Malcolm X. They were impassioned Americans who cast a harsh light on the truth of the inconsistencies and hypocrisy of our American credo "all men are equal," while challenging humanity to elevate themselves, and reject hate in favor of love and inclusivity.

JFK's tragic assassination in 1963 left Americans, and the world, stunned by the violent murder of a proactive voice. The 1960s were unquestionably turbulent; change was not a poster that everyone carried. The decade represented conflict against the status quo. It represented a country desperate to wrap its arms around a forgotten patriotism inspired by an assassinated president. It represented a vehement public outcry to disengage our troops from Vietnam. It represented a renewed commitment to civil rights, equality and peace. It also spawned the disturbing events that took the lives of great voices of change: JFK, Malcolm X, Martin Luther King, Jr. and Bobby Kennedy. These horrific assassinations are forever etched in the decade of the 1960s. These assassinations symbolize forces of power who wanted to silence forces for change. They are powerful moments that beg Americans to value historical perspective, and are meaningful for 2020 and what lies beyond.

How Did American Patriotism Change?

We lost our innocence. That is a simple answer, I know. The U.S. up to this point had spent over 190 years defending freedom for others and ourselves. Our patriotism carried a nationalist flag at times, and at other times, hand-written posters extolling change within our interior accompanied the American flag. We have repeated that course many times in our history. Vietnam was our entry into enduring wars. After Kennedy's assassination, the tone in the U.S. was flat. We were very vulnerable. If the inconceivable could happen, what could happen next?

The promise of the Great Society, Lyndon B. Johnson's dream, brought the focus back on repairing what was broken in our society. Twenty years of unprecedented economic growth brought societal affluence and a powerful middle class, but there was also a cost.

Systemic racism was alive in American suburban versus urban communities. Migration to the suburbs left decaying urban environments overrun with poverty. The inner cities had inferior public-school systems, and there was a strong need for jobs programs to elevate the unemployed out of poverty and into the work force. Chemical innovations in preserving the American food supply poisoned our waterways. A century of industrialization was polluting and depleting the beauty and the American natural resources that were so highly coveted by Western Europe during colonization.

We were an indulged society teetering on the precipice of destroying a great nation from the inside out. We were forgetting what the absolute priorities of our Founding Fathers were—not just protecting freedoms, not just defending our country, but also propelling our society forward. Lyndon B. Johnson's Great Society Speech, delivered at the University of Michigan shortly after JFK's assassination spoke to the attitude within American culture at that time:

> *"... a few years ago we were greatly concerned about the ugly American, today we must act to prevent an ugly America."*—
> LBJ's Great Society Speech, University of Michigan

Many of LBJ's goals for the Great Society still live with us today. His vision took the focus off growing an economy and keeping a watchful eye on geopolitics, to creating the substance within our society that benefits all people. The Great Society was not focused on a redistribution of wealth, or private philanthropy. The Great Society gave birth to government programs that subsidized the War on Poverty, Jobs Corp, Public Education, the Arts, and the environment and consumer safety. These programs were intended to enhance the very essence of what American freedoms and opportunity represent. The Great Society programs were initiated to help people out of poverty, to provide a clean, safe environment, and to give education and employment opportunities to those who had none. The ideals of these programs were to give a population of poverty a more level playing field to achieve independent success and become contributing members of American society.

These programs achieved so many aspects of LBJ's vision for a great society and most are still in effect today. The Office of Economic Opportunity is one of the prime examples of an entity created with multiple programs housed within to offer solutions to LBJ's "War on Poverty." The OEO and the Community Services Administration were to work in concert to achieve their goals of education, health, welfare and employment. Administrations came and went while these programs changed reporting structure, encountered massive cost over-runs, as well as federal and state jurisdiction issues resulting in fractured programs landing under State control. The programs still in existence morphed in size and scope over years and decades to the extent that they no longer resemble the original intent of the program—to help people help themselves.

Robert Woodson was born into poverty in the late 1930s. He is one of five children and was raised by a single mother. He enlisted in the U.S. Air Force and put himself through college. His early involvement in the Civil Rights Movement led to pioneering national community develop-ment programs. His mission pivoted in the late 1970s toward programs that advocated for low-income neighborhoods and empowered resi-dents through "self-help" rather than government assistance. Woodson's career has spanned sixty years from the National Urban League, the Center for Neighborhood Enterprise to the Woodson Center. He has authored hundreds of articles on poverty and self-empowerment.

Woodson recently described the reality of the government-funded programs developed to provide assistance to at-risk and low-in-come neighborhoods:

> One of the great promises we gave to low-income blacks is that if you were to elect blacks to public office through the Voting Rights Act and we were running those institutions, that all of black America would be better off. In the past 50 years 22 trillion dollars have been spent on the poverty programs.

Seventy percent goes not to the poor but to those who serve poor people. So, many of those people taking office use this money to create a class of people who are running these cities, and now ... we have all of these inequities. We have race being used as a ruse, as a means of deflecting attention away from critical questions, such as why are poor blacks failing in systems run by their own people? If we continue to look at life through a racial prism where evil wears a black face it will escape detection and therefore correction. How damaging is it to our society for leaders to effectively incite racial division and hatred in order to cover their own failures that seems like a very reckless thing to do ...

The Great Society was not intended to create a bureaucratic system with landfills of red tape and huge government organizations that enabled poverty. We continue to live with programs that are not directly benefiting the people they serve. Instead, these programs become place markers for power. They become useful politically through the threat of losing them. Ask the taboo question—who is being "served"?

It is instinctively American to empower each individual, not to create a victim mentality for the masses. The net result of many of the Great Society programs was an infrastructure that was designed to help but that would be exploited by multiple parties. This massive new infrastructure changed American patriotism as did the devastation of losing our 1960s American heroes. There was a feeling of hopelessness that permeated the country with the murders of icons that stood for change, empowerment and positive speech.

A societal change began to emerge that left motivation and empowerment at the door. These ideals were replaced with government sponsored entitlements benefiting Americans that were not incentivized to enter the work force. This did not improve our inner cities; poverty remained in the projects—<u>built</u> to house poverty.

A new mantra entered the American lexicon:

What can my country do for me, rather than what can I do for my country?

What can others do for me, rather than what can I do for others?

A Sinking Ship on Dry Land

Time was moving fast, and Americans were caught in a wave of societal change whose force was swift and emotionally turbulent. We were questioning our values, our patriotism, our Government, and we were forgetting how we got here. After a decade of lost heroes, the 1969 Moon Walk was a moment of disbelief and lump-in-the-throat American pride. During the summer of 1969, Americans watched Neil Armstrong take his first steps on the moon from televisions in the comfort of their living rooms. Not only did we have the technology to put a man on the moon, but we had a standard of living in our country that allowed a majority of Americans to watch this monumental event on TV, in their own homes. This was an extraordinary event for human achievement, but it represented far more to our country for that time. We were in the midst of fighting Communist expansion, the

Vietnam War and a Space Race with the Soviet Union. The Moon Walk gave every American a renewed sense of forgotten pride and hope. Astronauts were the new American heroes.

The country persevered during the 1970s—barely. Distrust and apathy were rampant. Americans were angry with the government and with our laws of equality. The Great Society programs had transformed into unwieldy programs that cost the country financially. We were fighting the Vietnam War at a cost to the country both financially and emotionally. Protests spilled over ongoing racial divisions, women's rights and acceptance of gay and lesbian couples. Inflation was the highest it had been since WWII. Gone were the days of prosperity of the previous two decades. Unemployment was extremely high, and interest rates were north of 20%, a number unimaginable to us today.

The oil embargo left Americans with a fuel shortage and sky-high prices to fill the gas tank. I can remember waiting in gas lines with my mom and my sisters. We sat in my mom's Ford Pinto in lines that seemed like an eternity just to pump gas. We had "odd and even days" for purchasing gasoline determined by the last digit on your license plate. It was the circumstance for my generation that would most resemble food rationing during my grandmother's generation 30 years earlier.

Watergate and the subsequent impeachment of Richard Nixon were other moments of a crumbling American society that represented failure. We'd lost our way; our apathy gave way to elected officials that represented a disenfranchised government.

Where Do We Go from Here?

This is an important question for the late 1970s and 1980s that carries the same relevancy today. There was a core shift in the 1960s that still drives American society, our expectations from our government and how politics play out in America today. That shift occurred with a sustained prosperity. We gathered strength to reaffirm that injustices still existed in enviable America through the Civil Rights Movement, the Equal Rights Movement, and the Gay Rights Movement. The Environmental Protection Agency gained prominence as polluted air and poisoned land and water became ugly realities of our American landscape. The same issues visit American life today. Social injustice requires vigilance. Balance of power encourages fair and reasonable paths to solutions.

From the end of World Wars to now, Americans have shifted from patriotism of "we" to "us vs. them" within our own country. Patriotism has become defined by political party affiliation. Revisit the history lesson of the weaknesses of the Articles of Confederation, as our country is no longer defined by geographic region, but by each State being referred to as either a "red" or a "blue" state. Where is the unity in this new way of describing a State's culture? What does it say about our willingness to allow words that alienate become accepted part of dialogue?

We have achieved a history over the last fifty years of extremes. If we refuse to recognize and understand these shifts, we cannot truly understand the histories we revisit nor escape repeating them. They are the result of the ebb and flow of good and bad economies. They are the result of the demand for societal improvement. They are the result of war, aggression and suppression.

LBJ's Great Society sought to take an already comfortable American society and encourages it to elevate humanity. The determination to focus efforts on these ideas left the American economy without a guidepost for sustainability, much less growth. Amid the 1970s inflation, recession, joblessness and government turmoil, there was little doubt that the country required a change in leadership. The Reagan era of the 1980s sought to rebalance the American economy so that the society could continue to exist. Economic and political shifts are not always perfect; they don't always benefit everyone or align with everyone's priorities.

Less government, deregulation and the dismantling of inefficient programs lowered interest rates, increased jobs and reaffirmed faith in the American economy and a better quality of life. Geopolitics embraced détente as a firm stand on any increased shifts of power within the Soviet Union's grasp. A looming Communist threat was a way of life for over 30 years in the U.S. The Soviets elected Gorbachev, who was a political reformer. This presented an opportunity for a new relationship with the West. Reagan gave his famous Berlin Wall speech in 1987, and less than 18 months later the Berlin Wall fell, tipping off a domino effect throughout Eastern Europe.

The Revolution of 1989 repeated a similar pattern from two centuries prior in France, where the French Revolution, fueled by the American Revolution, fought for freedom from sovereignty and tyranny. Poland, Hungary, East Germany, Bulgaria, Czechoslovakia,

Romania, Yugoslavia and Albania followed in the footsteps of Berlin. Within two years the Soviet Union would dissolve, and a free Russia would reemerge along with eleven new countries. The map of Eastern Europe and Russia was redrawn.

That same year the Tiananmen Square protests attempted a revolution against a Communist China regime. After several weeks of protest demonstrations, on June 4, 1989, Chinese troops entered Tiananmen Square and fired on civilians. It is estimated that roughly 10,000 people were arrested during and after the protests. Several dozen people were also executed for their role in the protests. An official death toll was never released by China. Eyewitness accounts from foreign diplomats state the death toll at Tiananmen alone was in the range of 2,600 to 2,700. Civilians were shot or bayoneted by military soldiers and run down by armored vehicles as described by foreign diplomats' witness to the horrific scene.

In 1989, I was a recent college graduate employed by a private label retail clothing company, fabricating garments in Hong Kong and China. Our merchandising department received faxes almost daily from manufacturers working 12 time zones away. The fax our offices received on the 6th of June 1989 was chilling. The author of the fax began to express the disbelief and shock of what was occurring. It was inconceivable. He spoke of the rapidly deteriorating situation: thousands were killed, students revolting, martial law and potential civil war. The national news in China only reported that the riot in Beijing's Tiananmen Square was cleared and resulted in no civilian fatalities, only injuries to soldiers. However, British-occupied Hong Kong residents had international news access. They watched live video reporting from correspondents for CBS, ABC and CNN before those international journalists were threatened and returned to Hong Kong.

Our Hong Kong affiliates relayed these stories to their mainland China counterparts and the heartbreaking realization set in that their government was lying to them. Hong Kong businesses began sending faxes and telexes to their associates in China trying to spread the truth of what happened. Every day students and Hong Kong citizens gathered at channels to China, such as rail stations, ferries and the airport to give newspapers to every passenger to hand carry to their friends and relatives in mainland China. They wanted the Chinese people to know the facts. The last words in the fax sent to my office said, "A people's revolution is expected soon." It failed, with China remaining a Communist country, advancing over the following 30 years to become a world superpower. What started as a protest for democracy, ended in a massacre.

The threat Communism presents today does not permeate the air the way it did 30 years ago . . . or does it? Somehow this feels different. How will it drive American patriotism? It is as important to pay attention to the realities of current events with the courage of our American convictions as it is to remember history. Politicians are concerned with the balance of trade internationally and especially with China. The globe is wide open in comparison to the closed Iron Curtain of 30–50 years ago. China's growing economy, unprecedented level of international trade, and the ability to offer products at extremely low cost should be a signal that America needs to change how we do business and prepare for greater self-reliance. The arrival of COVID-19 and the lack of transparency from a Communist regime during this global pandemic have put the entire world in jeopardy. Levels of trust and cooperation are tentative at best. This bears investigation, and Americans should require truth and transparency without conspiracy theory judgements or outcries of undiplomatic slander.

A very short timeline of actions and events speaks volumes in describing China's intentions. In 1997 Britain relinquished rule of Hong Kong to China in return for terms guaranteeing a 50-year extension of its capitalist system. In 2013 Xi Jinping came to power as President of China and immediately did away with term limitations granting him totalitarian rule over China indefinitely. His move to subdue democratic, free-market Hong Kong has been rapid. In June 2020 Xi instituted a Hong Kong Security Law which makes secession or subversion of the Chinese central government an offense punishable with life imprisonment. Protests in Hong Kong over the last year have become violent and deadly.

In the South China Sea, American aircraft carriers patrol the international waters as a reminder to the Chinese government that these are international waters. One third of the world's shipping trade passes through this region and the year Xi Jinping came to power, his government began building artificial islands on the reefs in violation of international environmental laws.

Along China's southwestern Himalayan region tensions at the India-China border have a long history of border dispute. Recently, these tensions have escalated resulting in the first fatalities at this heated border in 45 years. The move to take free-market Hong Kong does not bode well for free-market Taiwan's independence.

Where do we go from here, and how much do we value the core of the American way of life? Pay attention to history, because these events bear the markings of a historical repeat of totalitarian expansionist proportions that took hold of Germany and Western Europe in the 1930s.

The Millennial Effect

We have a new Millennial Generation, which has grown up in an affluent America similar to the Baby Boom Generation, and is larger in population than the Baby Boomers. Change is constant, but it does not prevent history from repeating itself. Technology, multimedia, Big Data and the Social Media Age have changed how we look at ourselves, the world, and our immediate access to information on almost any level. It has changed how we share information, how we interact with people, and it has increased our ability to collaborate with others.

We live in an increasingly divisive time, as we did 50 years ago. We are living in a global society that is assaulted with information. The immediacy of information, knowledge and communication has caused a stratospheric acceleration across industries, geographies and cultures. We cannot escape 24/7 information.

Immediate access to information—good or bad, real or fake—is at our fingertips every waking moment. The Information Revolution and the birth of the Digital Age have changed our economy, how we receive our information, how we perceive and protect our security, and ultimately how we think.

Behavioral marketing feeds advertising to internet consumers based on the websites they visit and the purchases they make. The content we receive in our newsfeed is sometimes based on elected preferences, but content is also "pushed" to us based again on what we have been reading or viewing. Big Brother is watching. The internet, YouTube videos and smart phones have changed a world that used to listen to "fireside chats" on the radio after the family evening meal. Today it's high-speed internet that allows the flow of information and the amount of information we receive to infinitely multiply from the days of radio or even the three network channels we watched on TV in the 60s and 70s. Add the mobile smart phone and social media outlets and the barrage of information becomes compounded to epic proportions.

A numbing effect occurs with the rapid-fire news cycle and convenience of technology at our fingertips. The public is not unmasking the chaos-driven events that encourage alienation, division, and thrive on short attention spans. Chaos thrives when we are diverted from the truth. Chaos achieves its goal when we as a society fall prey to the mayhem of the clash of wills and presentism, rather than embracing insight, intellect and perspective.

Dystopic Nuance

We are at a place in American history when we have two massive generations that have driven and will continue to drive the economy, politics and patriotism in this country. The Boomers are bringing up the rear with the youngest turning 56 in 2020. We were raised in an American environment that enjoyed the first sustained affluence within the American middle class. The Millennials, as offspring of the Baby Boomers, enjoyed a continuation of the same. Interestingly, both generations have grown up amidst a wave of dystopic literature. Novels such as 1984, Brave New World, The Handmaid's Tale, The Hunger Games and Maze Runner provide the backdrops for the cautionary tales of collectivism, socialism, totalitarianism and fascism in alternate worlds in which every human action is controlled and watched by the state.

The Pledge of Allegiance can have an awkward place in American patriotism today given the tenor of dystopic blind obedience it can suggest. Boomers grew up with this rote conformity, and for the most part have just accepted the Pledge as part of our patriotic heritage. Just as young Americans unquestioningly prepared for emergency drills, taking shelter under our elementary school desks during the 1970s.

"The Pledge" was actually written by Captain George Balch, a Union Army officer during the Civil War. After the war, he went on to teach patriotism in New York City schools. *This bears repeating*: Patriotism was a subject taught in American public schools. How would a patriotism class taught in the public school system feel to 2020 parents and their children? We have a very different society today, and a patriotism class might be considered centralized obedience.

The Pledge of Allegiance, as it became known, was more closely adapted from Francis Bellamy's pledge, a Baptist socialist minister. It was not formally adopted by Congress until 1945. In 1954, the words "under God" were added at the insistence of President Eisenhower. The Pledge became an opening recitation for government meetings as well as public schools in most States. The Pledge of Allegiance has a legally challenging history, as it has been called into question over idolatry—pledging to a flag. The pledge has also been accused of religious preference and some consider its mandatory recitation a "brainwashing" exercise. These same calls to allegiance are peppered through the history of Nazi Germany and the former Soviet Union. It seems strange and ironic, particularly because the Pledge became a "declared" allegiance in a country of freedoms.

The Millennials, now our largest generation, see the Pledge as "Jingoistic." They are watching fictional dystopia unfold on the screen with The Handmaid's Tale, Divergent and The Hunger Games, just as they read these same novels in school. They have a point.

Social media influenced this generation from the time they were in high school. They are environmentally "wired" for information and have grown up with a global social presence. They are collaborative, inclusive and self-expressive. Millennials also grew up with 9/11 and the Iraq War, and are the most ethnically diverse generation in American history.

This is a generation that has changed how we go about our daily life processes: they did not grow up on soda like the "Pepsi generation". Companies such as Coke and Pepsi have had to do a massive shift in product development to stay relevant and afloat in a millennial world of designer water and craft cocktails.

Telecommuting became prominent as Millennials hit the work force. This generation tagged the "foodie" label. They are looking for good, high quality food sources and restaurants. Farmers' markets are on the rise. Millennial parents have enacted change in public school system menus to reflect better, healthier choices for their children. They are hard workers and have driven technology to a place we've never imagined, with the ability to share, purchase and work, and all while on vacation from the convenience of our laptops. The new billionaires are Millennials that run companies like Facebook, WeWork and Airbnb.

How has this changed American patriotism? Baby Boomers seem to have fallen more in line with a deeper nationalistic pride that was reflected through the experiences of their parents and grandparents. Millennials drive a shift in American patriotism that is more culturally social in nature. Adult Boomers came away from 9/11 with feelings of distrust and disbelief and a more cautious nature. In contrast, Millennial children came away from that horrific event with an attitude of more inclusivity rather than isolationism.

Boomers waited for an invitation for a seat at the "grown-up table," while the Millennial approach has been to simply pull up a chair. The Millennial brand is to guide the rest of society to move and thrive in the midst of rapid change through positive experiences.

A New Emerging American Patriot

American pro-football player Colin Kaepernick famously defied a traditional patriotic act by not standing for the national anthem at the opening of a 2016 NFL game as a statement to raise awareness of racism and police brutality. It was a peaceful protest.

Did public reaction to his "statement" merit the outcome? His act of defiance was vilified, his career tarnished. He was using his First

Amendment rights as an American. We need to tread lightly on how we view freedoms in other countries, when we are so quick to judge the freedoms in our own country. If the shift in American patriotism means peaceful protest rather than violent rioting or shutting down speakers at college campuses—then Colin Kaepernick is on to something that achieves a more evolved and enduring reform and call to change—a model for conveying the courage of one's convictions, peacefully and humbly.

This is where we could revisit the word "détente" and the ability to ease tensions through diplomatic communication and use it within the context of our own society; Colin Kaepernick is a great example. His choices are his to make. Kaepernick has the freedom within our American society that celebrates individualism to do so. He knelt during the anthem to draw attention to real societal issues. The divisiveness seen on the news and reality TV were now invading entertainment. People and the news media were at odds over it. The repercussions for the NFL, his employer, were significant. Attendance at NFL games suffered that season, as did their network ratings. It hurt the franchise.

I don't believe it was Colin Kaepernick's intention to hurt the NFL franchise. But did his actions enact the change intended? Here we are in 2020, greater racial unrest than ever and nothing has changed—except that Colin Kaepernick's career suffered. We have not moved society forward on the issue of racial injustice. If that event during the 2016 football season occurred during the 2020 football season would there have been the same reaction by the NFL in terms of making a statement on how players should conduct themselves during their professional events?

Is it more legitimate and authentic to lend celebrity and voice to a Public Service Announcement, or to volunteer and lend celebrity to an organization—to put some time in to whatever is a real issue to the individual? The reality is that viewership is strongest during the sporting event where reaction has the most impact.

Perhaps we need to resurrect an old Cold War phrase and deploy it for an American interior that has respect for others. Détente—thoughtful guidance of our actions to solve our common problems peacefully and meaningfully. One person's impact not falling in line with the establishment in a show of reverence for an institution that avoids and minimizes glaring inequalities is powerful.

CHAPTER 10

The Impact of Population on Society

Mitigating factors create compelling evidence. We cannot bash our patrimony or reform it without examining historical perspective—and the big white elephant in the room—POPULATION. *Population has changed everything.* It has changed life in the U.S. and globally. It is very difficult to maintain "status quo" in the throes of massive population increases and density over the last century. Here are a few staggering statistics:

- According to the World Bank, the largest world populations are in the following countries with over **209 million people** living in each country: China (1.386B), India (1.339B), United States (325.7M), Indonesia (262.2M) and Brazil (212.2M).

- World Population has gone from 3.032 billion in 1960, to 7.53 billion in 2017. In 57 years, world population has increased 4.498 billion—**More than doubled, or a 148% increase in the world's population.**

- "It took over 200,000 years of human history for the world's population to reach 1 billion, and only 200 years more to reach 7 billion" —*PBS NewsHour*, 27 October 2011.

Taking that information into account should give clear perspective—hopefully inspiring mindfulness and rational thought—as to how we navigate our own patrimony and our mission statement as Americans.

Population and Crime

Look at crime and population, because it is a hot button. Fighting crime and the safety of the American population have been a huge focus during national and local election seasons and always will be. We all want to feel safe in our cities and our neighborhoods. We want a good quality of life for our children. We want our aging parents to be safe. Increased population brings increased crime, right? Not necessarily. According to a Pew Research Center report, violent crime in the U.S. has declined substantially in the last 25 years:

The two most commonly cited sources of crime statistics in the U.S. both show a substantial decline in the violent crime rate since it peaked in the early 1990s. One is an annual report by the FBI of serious crimes reported to police in approximately 18,000 jurisdictions around the country. The other is an annual survey of more than 90,000 households conducted by the Bureau of Justice Statistics. This study surveyed approximately 160,000 Americans ages 12 and older whether they were victims of crime, regardless of whether they reported those crimes to the police. Using the FBI numbers, the violent crime rate fell 49% between 1993 and 2017. Using the BJS data, the rate fell 74% during that span. (For both studies, 2017 is the most recent full year of data.) The long-term decline in violent crime hasn't been uninterrupted, though. The FBI, for instance, reported increases in the violent crime rate between 2004 and 2006 and again between 2014 and 2016.

We can't register complaint with a sitting president or political party for either of those two-year crime increases as they happened under G.W. Bush and Barack Obama respectively. More data from the Pew Research statistics on crime found the same sharp decline is seen in the property crime rate:

"Property crime has declined significantly over the long term. Like the violent crime rate, the U.S. property crime rate today is far below its peak level. FBI data show that the rate fell by 50% between 1993 and 2017, while BJS reports a decline of 69% during that span. Property crime includes offenses such as burglary, theft and motor vehicle theft, and it is generally far more common than violent crime."

That said, we do know geographic location rather than population affects the crime rate. Another statistic from the FBI, illustrating several states with lower populations:

"In 2017, there were <u>more than 600 violent crimes per 100,000 residents</u> in Alaska, New Mexico and Tennessee.

By contrast, Maine, New Hampshire and Vermont had rates below 200 violent crimes per 100,000 residents."

We have all experienced news stories on the rising and horrifying crime rates in Chicago, but here's another interesting statistic from the same study: "Chicago's murder *rate* in 2017—24.1 murders and non-negligent manslaughters per 100,000 residents—was less than half of the rates in St. Louis (66.1 per 100,000) and Baltimore (55.8 per 100,000)."

Are these crime statistics a surprise to you? There is so much daily news coverage of crime that it is no wonder we either become desensitized or fearful. The assault of news comes in so many forms: TV, laptops, mobile devices and tablets. News and information can be accessed from anywhere we have a Wi-Fi connection. Coincidence occurs along with the perception of a rising crime rate: the election cycle. Making our streets, our neighborhoods, our cities and our country safer is a huge piece of a candidate's campaign promises. Everyone wants to feel safe, right? Of course we do, and every candidate knows that is a campaign issue that drives home the vote.

Contrasted to the statistics stated above, most Americans by June 2020 would disagree that crime and violence are not on the rise today. This is where presentism may take over rather than perspective. There are groups all over the U.S. attempting to peacefully and intelligently protest the importance of *change now* with on point messages of inequities. There are also groups attempting to hijack the message by inciting volunteers to anger and violence, igniting fear in the lives of others. This becomes a diversion of chaos that accomplishes several goals: It allows election year politicians (election win) and the news media (ratings) to amplify a scene of a society perched on the precipice of disaster. It pushes the protests that convey a sincere desire to address inequities as a *peaceful* community off the airways. It ignites a mentality of followers rather than thinker and leaders. The resulting escalation in crime becomes anarchy's entitlement to disfigure society through violence and petty theft rather than reason and intellect.

I am certainly not trying to minimize horrific crimes, and I feel very strongly in the importance of highlighting violent crimes to raise awareness and vigilance—not to make us paranoid and guarded human beings. We do not want to lose our ability to be rational, considerate people. An informed public should be an empowered public, not a public smothered in hate and distrust. I use the examples of real data from Pew Research, whose statistics come from the FBI and the Bureau of Justice Statistics, to illustrate a recurring message I hope to get across in this book: Think. Investigate the veracity of your news sources and seek information from more than one source.

Racism and Crime

The conversation about crime does not end with the level of crime we are experiencing in the U.S. Racial profiling and abuse of power have been inadequately addressed in terms of how we view crime and incarceration in America. This issue is a whole separate conversation from the crime statistics represented above. We have a broken system that incarcerates unfairly and subsequently feeds the largest prison system in the world.

As Americans, we need to be open to educating ourselves not just on general crime statistics, but how our legal system has molded judicial process and a Gotham-sized prison system. We cannot address crime in our country appropriately without pointing out the tremendous flaws in our justice system in regard to systemic racism. Tell the truth. Be prepared to hear the ugly truth. This will not change unless Americans look in the mirror, acknowledge the wrongs, and commit to making it right. This will not change unless all of us call out racism and injustice in any scenario we witness.

When Americans collectively stand up against profiling a human being, based on race or religious affiliation, we will have a chance at success in changing a broken system, demanding equitable laws and judicial process. Americans need to accept the facts exhibited in real statistics that show that our system has incarcerated innocent people for life sentences. We have significant racial disparity in prison sentences in general.

A 2017 *Washington Post* article by Christopher Ingraham offers compelling facts from credible sources:

> Black men who commit the same crimes as white men receive federal prison sentences that are, on average, nearly 20 percent longer, according to a new report on sentencing disparities from the United States Sentencing Commission (USSC). These disparities were observed "after controlling for a wide variety of sentencing factors," including age, education, citizenship, weapon possession and prior criminal history.

Christopher Ingraham's article goes further to illustrate the changes in legal precedence that have enabled judicial autonomy, and contributed to abuse of power within the federal courts. A decision by the Supreme Court in 2005, <u>Unites States vs. Booker</u> demonstrates this:

> The Supreme Court gave federal judges significantly more discretion on sentencing by making it easier to impose harsher or more lenient sentences than the USSC's sentencing guidelines called for. Before that decision, federal judges were generally required to abide by those sentencing guidelines . . . A 2014 University of Michigan Law School study, for instance, found that <u>all other factors being equal</u>, black offenders were 75 percent more likely to face a charge carrying a mandatory minimum sentence than a white offender who committed the same crime.

The same 2017 Washington Post article, concludes with research from The Word Prison Brief and the USSC, citing statistics on the scale of systemic racial disparity, along with the colossal size of the prison system in America. The prison system in the U.S. has become BIG business and cannot be ignored, as it suggests that racial bias and increased incarcerations has contributed to the magnitude of the prison system.

> The United States currently houses the world's largest prison population, with an incarceration rate of roughly 666 inmates per 100,000 people. Among whites, the rate is 450 inmates per 100,000 people. The incarceration rate for blacks is over five times higher, at 2,306 inmates per 100,000 people. . . .

The USSC report indicates that sentencing decisions are a big driver of those numbers. And according to the University of Michigan study, at the federal level alone simply eliminating the sentencing disparity would reduce the number of black men in federal prisons by about 9 percent and save taxpayers at least $230 million a year.

In understanding population and crime there is eye-opening evidence that this form of subjugation in American democracy has created a substantial prison industry within our economy.

Population and the Environment

"You just notice how thin the atmosphere is, how fragile it looks, and that, combined with large swaths of pollution is somewhat alarming. We've got to take care of the environment" —American Astronaut Scott Kelly observing Earth from Space.

That statement gives perspective to how small the world can seem when there is the ability to visualize it in its entirety. It carries tremendous weight considering *who* said it, and *where* he was when he observed it. Listening to Astronaut Scott Kelly speak at the Richmond Forum , this man of science has not only performed scientific tests resulting in credible data, but also has been an eyewitness to a vantage point that 99.99% of us will never see firsthand. During his talk that evening he described that over the course of many years and several trips into space he observed numerous environmental impacts and changes: pollution in parts of Asia, wildfires in California, as well as the notably thin atmosphere.

We know the United States is the third largest population on the planet behind China and India. China and India have tremendous pollution and environmental issues. The U.S. population is less than a quarter of the size of each one of China or India's populations. However, the U.S. is about three times the geographical size of India. The United States and China are actually about the same size geographically. This may sound like good news, but as stewards of planet Earth we have an obligation to be environmentally responsible. It is that simple.

The American model of democracy and freedom are replicated around the globe. We need to—and we can do—the same for the environment. The environment and world population should concern us as Americans. We all breathe the same air. We all have a stake in what happens to our natural resources. A huge part of our American heritage is our phenomenal geography.

The United States benchmarked the creation of the world's first national park with President Ulysses S. Grant signing the Yellowstone National Park Protection Act in 1872. We are so fortunate, by birthright, to be living in a country that has the geographic diversity and majesty that it does. We should be proud of the National Park system we have, oceans and gulfs that surround 75% of our land mass. The tremendous number of beautiful lakes, rivers and majestic mountains that make up our country are astounding. People come from all over the world to enjoy and experience the beauty of nature in America. It is a true statement that as our national and global population increases, so does our carbon footprint.

Patriotism, at its heart, involves respecting and protecting the culture and country we love—and that includes our environment. Part of the American culture IS our amazing geography. We've had so many "wake up calls" where progress and industry have wreaked havoc on our environment, our quality of life and ultimately our health.

A Sobering Short List:

- *Bunker Hill Mine, Silver Valley, Idaho*—estimates are that over an almost 80-year period of time (1880s–1960s) it dumped 75 million tons of toxic sludge, containing lead, zinc, arsenic and cadmium, into Lake Coeur d'Alene, making the water toxic to animals and humans.

- *The North St. Louis suburbs*—where radioactive material— uranium, thorium and radium—was buried in a landfill in the 1940s. Remember the Manhattan Project from WWII? Residents in these towns claim that because of this contamination many people in the area have contracted cancer, auto-immune disorders and suffered birth defects.

- *Bridgeton, Missouri*—where 47,000 tons of nuclear waste was illegally dumped in the West Lake landfill. Eventually, in 1990, this area became an Environmental Protection Agency (EPA) Superfund site. Since at least 2010, an uncontrolled, under-ground fire has been moving toward this landfill, a potential calamity since the fire could burn the radioactive waste, send-ing toxic particles airborne, contaminating other local areas, including, perhaps, the nearby Missouri River. There is about

1,200 feet that separates the underground smoldering embers from the radioactive waste. A plan to avoid this potential calamity was finally developed five years later in 2015.

- *Mississippi Delta Dead Zone*—The run-off of chemical fertilizers dumped incredible amounts of nitrogen and phosphates into rivers such as the Mississippi, creating hypoxic areas known as dead zones. Algae propagate in these areas, killing fish and other marine life. "In the Mississippi Delta region of the Gulf of Mexico, this monstrous, suffocating discharge of chemicals and the resultant algal blooms cover some six to eight thousand square miles (the size of some states in the eastern U.S). Scientists at the National Oceanic and Atmospheric Administration and the Environmental Protection Agency have hoped to reduce the size of this dead zone to about 2,000 square miles, but this hasn't happened. The use of chemical fertilizers to produce corn and soybeans is the biggest problem in this regard, so unless American farmers grow considerably less and/or convert to organic farming, the Mississippi Delta Dead Zone will probably get larger in the coming years and decades." —*Kelley Marks, www. owlcation.com*

- *Love Canal-Niagara Falls, NY*—the Hooker Chemical Company (now Occidental Petroleum) buried 21,000 tons of toxic waste in the Love Canal section of Niagara Falls, New York.

- *Three Mile Island, Dauphin County*—nuclear reactor meltdown.

- *Exxon Valdez Oil Spill, Prince William Sound, Alaska*—the accident dumped 11 million gallons of crude oil into the ocean (some estimates are as high as 25–32 million gallons). The spill covered over 11,000 square miles of ocean and 1,300 miles of coastline.

- *The Ringwood Mines Landfill Site is a 500-acre area located in Ringwood, New Jersey.* Owned by the Ford Motor Plant, in the late 1960s to early 1970s, the site was used for waste disposal for its nearby Mahwah, New Jersey, automobile assembly plant. This waste was mostly paint sludge, a toxic mix of various industrial chemicals and heavy metals, which polluted the environment to the point that the Environmental Protection Agency (EPA) designated the area as a Superfund site in need of remediation, which began in 1984. By 2011, over 47,000 tons of contaminated earth were removed from the site.

- *Picher, Oklahoma* was one of the biggest mining towns in the country, dating back to the early 1900s. "Lead and zinc were mined there, 20 billion dollars' worth from 1917 to 1947. Toxic waste piled up in Picher, and the waterways in the area turned reddish brown. In 1996, investigators discovered that 34 per cent of the children in Picher had lead poisoning, mainly because lead had contaminated the ground water. In 2009, the state of Oklahoma "dis-incorporated" the town of Picher and, with the help of federal money, people began moving away. Picher is now a ghost town and considered one of the most toxic places in the U.S." —*Kelley Marks, www. owlcation.com*

- **BP Oil Spill, Gulf of Mexico**—an oil rig explosion, the damaged rig leaked oil into the ocean for 87 days, and spilled an estimated 210 million gallons of crude oil into the sea.

- *The U.S. and the Soviet Union Cold War*—a time when both sides tested numerous nuclear devices. Initially, the U.S. exploded its bombs in the South Pacific, and then in January 1951 they began nuclear testing at the Nevada Test Site in southern Nevada. "At times, the mushroom clouds from these detonations could be seen in the city of Las Vegas, only 65 miles from the site. *Parts of Nevada, Arizona and Utah* had radioactive fallout sprinkled upon its residents for years during the atmospheric tests. St. George in southern Utah may have gotten the worst of the fallout, because it was downwind of the test site. In fact, a John Wayne movie, The Conqueror, was filmed around St. George when a bomb nick-named "Dirty Harry" was exploded, and afterwards the film's cast and crew experienced an unusually high rate of cancer. Furthermore, deaths from various forms of cancer increased in the test site area from the middle 1950s into the 1980s. After testing at the site ended in 1992, the Department of Energy estimated that 300 megacuries of radioactivity remain at the site, making it the most radioactive place in the U.S." —*Kelley*

Marks, www.owlcation.com. [It should be noted for scale that as small a measurement as one *milli*curie can be fatal.]

- ***Flint, Michigan***—insufficient water treatment exposing dangerously high lead levels in drinking water. Between 6,000 and 12,000 children were exposed to high levels of lead in the drinking water.

Our patrimony should not be consumer driven to the point of environmental ignorance. We are so fortunate, as Americans, to have the geographically diverse country that we live in. Our country and the Earth deserve respect and admiration. The best gifts we can give are the efforts to ensure it remains a place of beauty brimming with natural resources.

While Americans are far more environmentally conscious than in prior decades, our basic awareness of recycling needs re-education. Our day to day consumption is staggering. The rise in disposable products is facilitated by manufacturers who lull the public into accepting that disposable always equal recyclable. That is not true.

Not all plastics are created equal in terms of recycling. An estimated 25% of recycled materials are contaminated, meaning they have not been adequately rinsed and cleaned of debris and greases. In most cases, if something as simple as a cardboard pizza box has pizza oil stain on it, it cannot be recycled. Rules for recycling vary State to State and even county to county. Understand what the pesticides and fertilizers are doing to your soil, water run-off and how you are tracking it into your homes. Understand your local legislation in play before congress impacts your mountains, rivers, bays and streams.

Sustainability holds great potential for the environment's future . I'll share an American good news story moving the ball forward on the field of environmental action with purpose and serving multiple needs. COVANTA, a global energy-from-waste company: landfill waste. It is fascinating. COVANTA describes in their mission statement that *no waste is ever wasted*. Ever drive along the highway and see a towering landfill on the horizon and wonder how in the world we will ever absorb the amount of waste our world population creates? I do. I wanted to know more, and so I got in touch with someone at COVANTA.

I was taken through the evolution of the power industry and the fast-forward thinking toward wind power and electric vehicles. The potential for the power grid with its segmented vulnerability is likely destined to become a thing of the past. Not pole towers, but satellite communication, very much along the lines of the evolution of the landline to wireless telecom industry, will be commonplace in the energy industry.

What makes COVANTA unique is that they produce power by burning garbage, solid waste. The ash from burning the solid waste, which in turn is fueling the power, is collected in "bag houses," much like a vacuum bag filter. It is an air pollution control device and works to maintain a smaller footprint and emission controls. Ash management takes sustainability to the next level by using the contained ash from the bag houses for aggregate and asphalt.

Metals from the landfill are burned as well, separated by ferrous and nonferrous metals, and staged for resale in their respective markets.

In the U.S. COVANTA's largest concentration of facilities are on the northeast coast from Washington D.C. to Massachusetts with the most facilities in Florida. The company's big growth is actually overseas in Europe and China. In fact, their facilities map shows a second headquarters in Shanghai. European and Chinese markets still have a more forward-thinking renewable resource mentality than we do in the U.S.

Americans have the ingenuity and the technology to achieve the promise of a sustainable future. However, we have a special interests culture within our borders that has not embraced renewable energy the same way other countries have ... but we are showing others how to do it! How will we carry this forward?

Population and Immigration

Immigration becomes an issue with population and is a huge political topic in our current discourse. Our historical patrimony is a young country with open arms that welcomed foreign people to our land of opportunity:

> Give me your tired, your poor,
> Your huddled masses yearning to breathe free,
> The wretched refuse of your teeming shore.
> Send these, the homeless, tempest-tost to me,
> I lift my lamp beside the golden door!

—Excerpt from Emma Lazarus' Poem (1883) which is immortalized in bronze on the Statue of Liberty.

During the late 1880s the United States was still a young country. We had barely celebrated the centennial anniversary of the Declaration of Independence. The changes occurring during those 100 years were dramatic industrially, geographically and politically. The United States had an impressive land mass that was still a "new frontier" moving to the West, just as it was a new land to the first settlers of Jamestown in 1607 more than 250 years prior.

The population was ramping up, and as a country with a large geography, we could handle that explosive growth. If people were willing to work hard, live by rule of law and adopt the framework of the U.S. Constitution, they were most likely granted citizenship. Ellis Island was, from 1892 to 1924, America's largest and most active immigration station. Well over 12 million immigrants were processed through those doors. Ellis Island was referred to as the "island of hope" for so many eager to begin a new life in the land of opportunity, or the "island of tears" for the small percentage of those who were deported and denied entry.

The U.S. population between 1890–1925 grew from 62,979,766 to 115,829,000 people. In 2020, the U.S. population is approximately 330 million people. We have tripled in size in less than 100 years, living in the same geographic footprint. This is an important fact to consider when we look at crime, or the environment, or immigration and how it affects our economy, our prosperity and quality of life. We have "over the top" media coverage of the immigration process at our southern border. Images of the Statue of Liberty, Emma Lorenz' poem and Ellis Island turn of the century photographs often portray an idealized vision of immigration to the United States. Immigration by its very nature cannot be viewed through a rose-colored lens. The process is imperfect and always has been. Americans had a miniscule amount of news coverage during the Ellis Island years in comparison to what we see at our southern border today. Ellis Island has been romanticized, but it was anything but romantic. People came into the processing center sick with disease that they either brought with them or contracted on the ship crossing. Families were separated then, too.

Immigration is complicated and imperfect. Illness, disease, lack of work/labor skills were all reasons people were deported at Ellis Island. Many made it through, and some had to turn around and go back to their country. There was a vetting process at Ellis Island. The U.S. has at least six agencies that include the State Department and the Department of Homeland Security that weigh in on the immigration process in place today. With the population we have in the U.S. today, it makes sense that there are agencies that balance all parts of the immigration system. I am not implying that it does not need to improve. It is a characteristic of American patriotism and culture that process becomes progress when it remains on the conveyor belt of improvement.

We cannot ignore the emotional issues of immigration, children separated from their parents, and working with people seeking asylum. These are real issues of the immigration process needing to be appropriately addressed to ensure the safety and welfare of the people involved. If someone attempting to enter the U.S. is deported after going through a question and interview process that has been put in place to protect the country from potential issues, there is a good reason. If that person continues to remain in the U.S., they are breaking the law. Just as American citizens are supposed to be living by laws in this country, so should those who wish to live here. I'd like to see if most of those critical of immigration officials could do their job for a week or even a day. It is a TOUGH job.

We cannot continue to cry that our statements about our American core, with regard to immigration, is a falsehood, if we don't educate ourselves on the intricacies of immigration—or at the very least use common sense and rational thought rather than react over news stories and political banter. As citizens, we become the fools who react and get on board the "political bandwagon." Freedom of Press is an important part of our patriotic freedoms, but media outlets are in the business to sell news and increase ratings. Politicians are in the business of getting elected. Please do not forget that when you are deciphering what is playing out in any news story or political debate.

From a security standpoint, if American society lacks the proper immigration processes designed to protect American citizens, doesn't that increase the likelihood of the infiltration of terrorism or dangerous gangs? We have clear examples of Al Qaeda and ISIS operatives and MS-13 gang members who have entered illegally.

There are so many hard-working immigrants in this country who value life, liberty and the pursuit of happiness. However, there are also a small percentage of people who immigrate to the United States to denigrate the society we have built.

Diversity and tolerance build strength and intellect—as long as people want to come to this country for the right reasons, not to escape the law in their own country and then contribute to a lawless path in the United States.

Immigration should not allow for abuse of our welfare system, or offer a "camp out" in our economy without contributing to our economy. Immigration should not be an opportunity to gain free access to higher education in our country while legal American citizens work tirelessly to put their children through college, or their children are burdened with student loan debt to make it through college. These are just a few of the reasons why the vetting process makes common sense to create a fair and equitable path for immigration as well as for those who are naturalized citizens.

Come to this country to work, to contribute to the American society, to engage in American culture and raise your children to want to do the same. Come to this country to go through the same citizenry process as every legal citizen who has come before you. Understand that the land of opportunity is also the land of global responsibility. We have been the beacons and the benchmark for democracy. We have also become the world's police and we have been extremely benevolent financially around the world. Come to this country to contribute, but remember that world generosity comes at a price, and the price for America is that we teeter on the brink of social and economic ruin in our own great country when we spread ourselves thin for the rest of the world. At some point, that utopian ideal becomes a financial disaster and the prosperity and opportunity that defines the American Dream could vanish.

CHAPTER 11

The Evolution of American Political Parties

The U.S. Constitution did not provide for political parties. However, the formation of parties that represented the interests of the people was something that the Founding Fathers realized held merit. Political parties were seen as another opportunity for governmental "community outreach" to gauge the barometer of the people on issues pertaining to local and federal laws, and what ultimately became subsequent amendments to the Constitution.

The journey political parties have taken in this country, like most entities evolved over the centuries. The infancy of party history began with the Federalist Papers. The Federalist Papers written over the course of 1787 and 1788 defended the principles of the Constitution with the purpose of educating and persuading citizens to embrace and ratify the Constitution. We went from a rallying cry for revolution and freedom to the great debate over how we protect those freedoms.

There were two emerging schools of thought for and against certain articles of the Constitution. They were the Federalists and the Anti-Federalists. Federalists supported the Constitution. They believed that the Constitution limited government and not the people. Anti-Federalists were skeptical that the Constitution could withstand historical change without amendments that would limit the power of the government and ensure that public oppression did not occur. It all boiled down to these issues: <u>centralized government</u>, a risky proposal that provided the government with too much power and threatened States' sovereignty and <u>personal liberties</u>.

The compromise became the Bill of Rights. This gave the nation a document of core principles that outlined our democracy, along with a list of amendments of clarified changes to the Constitution. Why is this important? These documents practiced mindfulness. The Declaration of Independence was a clear persuasive argument of serious intent for freedom from Great Britain. It became an American mission statement. The Constitution was a hard-reasoned written document of serious intent to develop the core principles for a young republic and the framework for building a democracy. The Bill of Rights represented the efforts of impassioned people to remain stalwart in keeping the promise of individual liberties at the forefront of the formation of this country.

After the ratification of the Constitution and the election of the American republic's first president, George Washington, the Anti-Federalist movement evaporated and the formation of the Democratic-Republican party emerged. There was strong political push and pull, and the reactive behavior found when power struggle mingled with human nature. The issue of the role of government was very present, with the Federalists remaining the party of strong central government and a central banking system, while the Democratic-Republican party saw limited government as the best solution.

By the time Washington gave his farewell address, after serving as President for eight years, he saw the writing on the wall for political parties. Washington spoke of the importance of unity to preserve peace at home. He spoke of the importance of factions that held the Constitution to account, while describing the dangers of political parties that lure special interests and propagate divisiveness over bipartisanship and compromise.

We become our own worst enemy when we favor loyalty to party over loyalty to the nation. How incredibly profound Washington's words were and remain relevant over 200 years later. Every year since 1896, the U.S. senate observes George Washington's birthday by selecting a member of the Senate to read his farewell address. It is an annual reaffirmation of the spirit in which the elected body should be representing their constituency.

The Federalist Party was dominated by its most tireless advocate, Alexander Hamilton, a contrarian, appealing to the business and banking community. Famous Democratic-Republicans, like Thomas Jefferson and James Madison, were agrarians and their priorities were with agriculture and farming. The focus of the North was on business, banking and industry versus the focus of the South being agriculture, large plantations and slave labor.

Red Elephants and Blue Donkeys

After the war of 1812 the Federalist Party began to disappear and was replaced with the Whig Party led by Henry Clay, and the Democratic-Republican Party became the Democratic Party led by

Andrew Jackson. The Whigs took the Federalist stand on business, tariffs, rule of law, minority protections against majority tyranny and a strong central government. By the 1850s the Whig Party dissolved and the Republican Party emerged. The Democratic Party was in favor of States' rights (autonomy from the federal government), constitutional conventions, slavery, and after the Civil War, the opposition of civil and political rights for African Americans.

There was an increased interest in voting among the population. Political parties became more organized to attract voter loyalty through rallies and partisan newspapers. Record voter turnout ignited the fuel that gave political parties power.

Party Brand Irony and Partisanship

This century has branded each party in interesting terms. The Democratic Party supports liberalism: a word that suggests liberty—freedom. Egalitarianism, minority rights (which was an about-face from what the early Democratic party supported), religious and multi-cultural freedoms and sexual orientation rights—these speak to liberty. Protecting the environment is vital to sustain life in a world where we can enjoy these freedoms and appreciate beauty.

Strengthening social programs becomes the sticky wicket. Enlarging social programs enables a society to accept subjugation. Let me explain my statement: we are not free if our incomes, our taxes and our way of life are programmed by government entities. Reducing the special interest web of government spending and honing programs that create the most benefit to our society allow for fiscal responsibility. Guidelines that record metrics to determine the merit of these programs and define a program's success are vital, as well as the level they should continue to be funded.

The Republican Party supports lower taxes, free markets, deregulation and a strong national defense. These all speak to liberty as well. Both parties support principles and interests that encourage a thriving society. Partisan politics has stalled the efforts to achieve that balance for almost two decades.

Power Struggle is Blind to Insight, Reason and Problem Solving

"Under democracy one party always devotes its chief energies to trying to prove that the other party is unfit to rule—and both commonly succeed, and are right." —H.L. Mencken, American Journalist

Both parties speak to freedoms. Both parties have corruption. Both parties have hypocrisies. Both parties propagate hateful banter. Both parties are guilty of these behaviors, and as elected representatives on the state and national level, should find shame in their inability to conduct their elected office with decorum and compromise. The corruption of power and special interest agenda has fallen to an all-time low.

If lawmakers cannot arrive at bipartisan solutions, what does that model for their constituencies? The Constitution and the Bill of Rights were documents put in place by our Forefathers to encourage government representatives to work together to find a balance of power. Where has the emotional intelligence gone? Détente is a form of communication strategy we employ in international diplomatic circles, but we shun that same form of communication within national diplomacy—within our own borders.

We are at a time, not just in American history, but globally, when we need to sort out and problem solve together. Our country cannot afford to continue the message of hate and discord. This divisive narrative does nothing but tear the country apart. Political parties in power come and go. It is the historical repeat and ebb and flow of American politics. Politicians have become labeled as "not able to play well with others."

> *A politician is a fellow who will lay down* <u>your</u> *life for* <u>his</u> *country*—Texas Guinan, American Actress during the Prohibition Era.

Has anyone heard a politician say, "you spoke—and we listened?" Modern politics has become a conduit for special interests.

> *"In order to become the master, the politician poses as the servant"*—Charles de Gaulle.

Politicians are <u>telling</u> the public what the public <u>needs</u>, rather than humbly assuming the auspicious role of representing what the constituency wants. There are politicians in the U.S. that represent what used to be our greatest cities of culture and pride. Today those cities are decaying. These lawmakers have chosen to abandon their constituencies in favor of voraciously defending their political power stronghold in Washington D.C.

Understand that increasing government gives all of the power to lawmakers and less power to the people they serve. Beholden to the government for food, health care and financial assistance, people will always be subjects and lawmakers the sovereigns no matter the style of government.

> *"There will never be a really free and enlightened State until the State comes to recognize the individual as a higher and independent power"*—Henry David Thoreau.

Moving away from a tribal identity and returning to a national identity encourages an inclusive society. Patriotism as faith in country and each other does not come without really working together to realize common purpose and achieve common goals.

CHAPTER 12

The Endangered Freedoms of Bias

We live in a global environment that has an unprecedented level of information access with the ability to view that information, in real time. We can witness an active war zone from our electronic devices, in real time. Seventy-five years ago, we would have been looking at footage that was not in HD and was vetted to give hope and improve morale. Today, anyone can put information and images on the web, a potentially sharp, double-edged sword. Why? We have become desensitized. We have become numb. Events or scenes that used to be unthinkable lose their impact, their magnitude and their ramifications.

We have become a very reactionary society. We believe and react to everything we see or read. We do not fact check. We are raising a generation that has lived this from the time they were learning to read and develop tactile skills. I see more posts that go from zero (lifestyle influencer postings) to 60 (knee-jerk reactions and associated panic to current events) with nothing measured in between. This culture of idealistic self-expression has an inherent presentism: only the present exists. There is a void in the ability to communicate with reason and a higher level of <u>emotional</u> IQ. These are insights gained from perspective on history, human nature and philosophy.

The Allegory of Truth and Story

Long ago, *Truth* walked naked upon the earth. His body was strong and muscular. His skin was smooth and shining. He was beautiful.

Whenever he walked into a village, he would call out, "I am *Truth*! Come, gather around and listen to what I have to teach you."

No one would come and no one would gather around him. The village children's parents would usher them away, covering their eyes. Young women stared curiously, and then turned away. Young men were envious. Old women sighed, and old men were sad. All turned away from *Truth* as he walked naked down the street.

No one would linger to listen to *Truth*. He traveled from village to village, and it was the same everywhere he went.

One day he came to the place where his sister, *Story* lived. Her home was a large white house with a wide porch that wrapped around it. There were beautiful trees, ferns and flower gardens surrounding the house. On the porch were white wicker rockers with flowered cushions and wicker shades hanging from the porch roof. *Story's* home had lace curtains at the windows and the sunlight streaming through made rainbows on the carpets inside.

Story was sitting in one of the rockers on her wide front porch. She was wearing a flowing silk gown that shimmered with iridescent colors.

She had ribbons entwined in her long golden curls, jewels on her fingers and sparkling silver shoes. She saw her brother coming down the road and could see that he looked very dejected.

Story ran out to her brother and asked, "What is wrong, dear brother? Why do you look so sad? What can I do to help you?"

"Oh, *Story*," sighed frustrated and deflated *Truth*, "I have traveled from village to village to share what I know. Everyone turns away from me. It is the same wherever I go. I don't understand it. I have so many things to share. Why won't people listen?"

"Ah," said *Story*, "come inside. I believe I can help you."

Story took her brother into her home and opened closets, chests of drawers and trunks filled with colorful clothes and finery. She told *Truth* to dress himself up.

"Oh, I couldn't do that, I would look silly," *Truth* replied.

Story insisted, and so *Truth* reluctantly began to dress up. He put on a white silk shirt with billowing sleeves, purple velvet knickers, shiny shoes with a silver buckle and a quilted vest with jewels. He put rings on his fingers and a hat with a long curling feather on it. When *Truth* was finished, *Story* gave him a look over and added a flower in his lapel, a silk cape and a long flowing scarf. Now he was ready. Story told *Truth* to return to the villages and try to gather the villagers once more.

A year later, *Truth* returned to his sister's house. *Story* saw him coming down the road smiling and triumphant. "*Truth*, you look so happy, tell me what you experienced."

"*Story*, it was wonderful. Everywhere I went, people listened to me. They would gather around and sit for hours while I talked. But what I don't understand is that I wasn't telling them anything different from before. Why was it that they listened to me this time?"

"Ah, *Truth*, don't you understand? No one wants to hear the <u>naked truth</u>, but they will listen when it is <u>clothed in story</u>."

The News Media

In 1949, the Federal Communications Commission introduced a policy referred to as the Fairness Doctrine. The policy was put forth to require all broadcast licensed entities to (1) present the public with reporting on controversial issues and (2) do so in an honest, equitable and balanced way. The main objective of the Fairness Doctrine was to ensure viewers had exposure to a variety of viewpoints. The networks could then present these programs in a variety of ways such as editorials, current affairs or news programs. There were limited news channels at the time and the FCC felt the policy was a necessary step to achieving balance for American viewership.

The New Journalism Movement of the 1960–70s guided print news reporting in a new direction for its readership. It captured the reader's attention by delivering the facts in a story with the style that favored nonfictional writing. It abandoned the dry rendition of real-life events, for a story that conveyed the facts of real-life events with rich detail and emotion. The impact was immediate. It reengaged the reader. But, was it the beginning of the loss of objectivity? Did it inspire a movement toward journalistic bias?

In 1987, the Fairness Doctrine was repealed as being in conflict with Freedom of Speech. It was determined at that juncture in broadcast history that enough of a variety of media outlets existed in the marketplace. It was no longer relevant to the original intent of the policy where only a few news networks existed. It has been a matter of controversy. Repealing the doctrine was a matter of debate again in 2008, but did not receive support in Congress. Public opinion was equally mixed in support and opposition. While most Americans might not be aware of the Fairness Doctrine—and it is an important piece of journalistic evolution—the Doctrine's demise has been charged by some as being responsible for fueling political polarization.

What is the truth? I think most of us ask ourselves that question every day. It has taken time, and has crept into our daily news exposure incrementally over the decades, but there is a change so palpable that we, as viewers should not ignore it.

The press has gradually abdicated its role as the watchdog of our democracy, to such a degree that citizens cannot look to the press for impartial, informed critical information to enable Americans to make the best decisions in elections and otherwise. What is worse is that we as an electorate and as citizens have failed to demand more of the press. We have a 24-hour news cycle for very fast paced lifestyles.

We are not paying attention to how news outlets exist to play out biases to their audiences. What lens are you watching your news through? Are you watching the news that is making you feel good, or the most comfortable? Or, are you watching and reading a variety of news outlets to truly understand the level of bias that exists so that you can sort out the truth from story or angle? There are many unbiased sources to get your information from, and until we all start making the effort to make that a routine ritual, we will continue to develop as a society that is driven by emotional reaction, rather than educated reason.

Newspapers and news channels have become political party weapons. The dangers inherent in the saturation of party bias reporting are huge. We allow ourselves, as a population, to become followers instead of leaders. We become lemmings instead of individuals. We gradually lose sight of what our civil liberties are in this country, and the importance of defending them. Something with far-reaching implications is happening as well: the delineation of bias within our news media promotes a social mentality of division, intolerance and censorship.

Censorship is occurring when clips of news conferences are edited to fit the framework of an opposing agenda. Morning and nightly news have become cleverly crafted opinion segments. Journalistic "spin" is a direct hit to the audience's emotions. People buy into it. It sells. Spin implies something happened without the evidence of hard facts, quotes or witnesses to an event. It is journalism's reactive behavior to be the first to report in a 24-hour news cycle. There is an unfortunate mentality of the journalistic right to print or broadcast unsubstantiated claims AND to present opinion statements as fact. This is the hysterical, repetitive banter of sound bites and sensationalized stories. This method of reporting news now reaches far beyond the media, with our POTUS using social media to Tweet news and opinion. It takes away the freedom to make your own informed decisions and settles into the mind of the audience that if it is reported, it must be fact. It becomes difficult to navigate as a Freedom of Speech issue. As citizens we can learn to filter information. For example, does the information come from a reliable source, and is the source stating facts or opinion? Pay careful attention to words that indicate bias. A well-researched online resource for sorting out forms of bias can be found on www.allsides.com.

Journalistic Transparency and an Informed Public

The New Journalism Movement of 50 years ago has changed and shifted news reporting in some positive ways. It has encouraged a more exciting way of delivering the news. Audiences have a very difficult time staying with a dry news story. How a journalist delivers the story in a way that resonates with the audience is a balancing act. Journalists who develop a readership or viewership do so because of trust. The audience trusts them because they present information that is factual, they back it up with solid credibility and they convey a passion for what they are doing. The audience is affected by sincerity and earnest conviction. Or—the audience may simply just like the way *Truth* is dressed.

Journalism has also changed in the past half century in terms of deference to government officials. Is this a problem? I think we have to look at the psychology of how humans feel when their team is called into question. Is it biased reporting or is it that we don't like the messenger? Journalists have a responsibility to seek the truth and to hold government officials accountable. How that is demonstrated requires transparency from the media and the vigilance to articulate the story to the public in a way that does convey skepticism but serious intent to get to the truth.

Academia

American institutions of higher learning have generated great thinkers and innovators. Our colleges and universities attract great talent from all over the world. The American Ivy League has always stood as an example of American exceptionalism in higher learning. In the last 50 years that honor has trickled into our state universities and our small private colleges.

We have a higher education system that offers something for every individual in terms of size, geographic location, course of study and general lifestyle, but regrettably the price tag of this level of education can be elusive. We have gone from a higher education system post-WWII that gave opportunity to anyone serving in the military who could return home to a free education, and expanded that opportunity to offer scholarships that serve the American minority population today. For many, the fulfillment of the American Dream is the ability to make college accessible to all people.

Today that dream of higher education is in danger of disabling the fabric of our educated society within the Humanities. Universities are very motivated to increase research and development. Technology, innovation and prize money have command of the living room and the true essence of the Humanities is left waiting at the back door. Additionally, colleges and universities are remodeling campuses to resemble country clubs catering to wealthy families—potential donors—and the result appears to be an environment that focuses more on amenities than it does on the quality of education.

The focus in the Humanities classrooms is less on philosophies and the debates of historical or ethical significance and more along the lines of dogmatic bias. There is no longer the decorum of sharing different ideas and opinions, but instead a shouting down of opponents. Higher education is actually condemning freedoms such as speech and individuality. What does it say about the hypocrisy on campuses that value diversity of race, religion and ethnicity but do not value diversity of thought?

Quoted directly from the ACLU website:

The First Amendment to the Constitution protects speech no matter how offensive its content. Restrictions on speech by public colleges and universities amount to government censorship, in violation of the Constitution. Such restrictions deprive students of their right to invite speech they wish to hear, debate speech with which they disagree, and protest speech they find bigoted or offensive. An open society depends on liberal education, and the whole enterprise of liberal education is founded on the principle of free speech.

How much we value the right of free speech is put to its most severe test when the speaker is someone we disagree with most. Speech that deeply offends our morality or is hostile to our way of life warrants the same constitutional protection as other speech because the right of free speech is indivisible: When we grant the government the power to suppress controversial ideas, we are all subject to censorship by the state.

Protecting our civil liberties is paramount to preserving a free American society. We do not all have to agree, and by all means, protest against the issues you do not agree with. Develop a debatable argument, but be civil. Allow speakers of differing opinions. Be civil. Most speakers would most likely welcome the opportunity to not just speak in front of a group, but to also engage in a civil debate on their subject. Reason takes courage. Hate and suppression are the cowardice of a bully.

If we want to live in a civil society then we need to be civil to each other.

> *If the freedom of speech is taken away then dumb and silent we may be led, like sheep to the slaughter*—Martin Luther King, Jr.

As Americans it is our belief system to always strive to become better and to practice freedoms. As human beings we sometimes get in the way of our belief system.

CHAPTER 13

The Brilliance of Thomas Paine

English-born Thomas Paine did not step onto the shores of the British colonies until 1774, at 40 years of age. He was encouraged to immigrate to the colonies by no less than Benjamin Franklin himself, who saw obvious promise in Paine's ability to courageously convey his message in a relatable way through essay. What was remarkable about Thomas Paine was that he was able to understand his audience.

It did not matter that he was British. He wrote essays such as Rights of Man in defense of the French Revolution, and he wrote Age of Reason advocating reason and free thought and criticizing institutionalized religion. He had admirers and he had enemies. What no one can argue is that Thomas Paine and his essays sparked controversy during their day, inspired revolution and have provided timeless inspiration on the rights of human beings. He was a pioneer in human rights activism. He knew how to speak to what resonated with people. He did so with simple, direct language.

Common Sense

What could be plainer than common sense? Thomas Paine found language that spoke to the people with convincing delivery. His arguments were for independence from England and the creation of a democratic republic. His pamphlet was an instant bestseller that sold over 120,000 copies within three months, amongst a small population. In today's numbers, Common Sense represents one of the bestselling books of all time.

What's more is that Paine, not a religious man himself, knew his audience as God fearing and took full advantage of this using religious reference in his arguments. He also wrote Common Sense anonymously; no one knew it was actually written by a British emigre. While Thomas Jefferson worked and reworked drafts of what would become the Declaration of Independence, Common Sense ultimately drove the language in the spring of 1776. Common Sense inspired Jefferson's final draft of the Declaration of Independence to signing in July.

What was so compelling about Common Sense? It empowered the individual. Paine began his argument stating that society benefits from individual liberty, the self-governed, and that limited government is necessary to uphold the laws crafted by the citizenry to keep society safe and enduring. He was well organized and cited Biblical verses that would engage the respect of the audience he knew would accept Common Sense as an essay of empathy, empowerment and a call to action.

Paine identified two types of tyrants for his audience: monarchs and aristocrats. Focusing on the identified tyranny, he skillfully reminded his readers that passages from the Bible that predated monarchy spoke differently. The history of the Bible begins with all men equal at creation, and so the hierarchy among kings and commoners is untrue. He refutes divine rights, citing several passages from the Bible that substantiate his claim. Paine then moves into the absurdity for one man to collect large sums of money each year doing no work, while loyal subjects worship their king and toil for a substandard quality of life.

Lastly, he describes in detail a blueprint for creating a system that incorporates a Continental Charter as well as a framework for organizing representatives from each colony. Once he has delivered the realities of tyranny, and proposed a strategy to solve the problem, he finishes his argument with empowerment. He empowers the colonies by praising their military ability and promise.

Rights of Man

> "Independence is my happiness, and I view things as they are, without regard to place or person; my country is the world, and my religion is to do good"—**Thomas Paine,** Rights of Man.

Paine's words convey a humble attitude whose loyalties lie with humanity. It was 1792 and with a triumph realized for the American colonies in his argument for Common Sense, Thomas Paine sailed back to Europe and positioned himself in France amidst growing unrest. Paine became the civilized world's expatriate ambassador towards realizing true freedom and equality for all people. He planted the seeds that again inspired and empowered France to reject sovereign rule.

Rights of Man was intended as a collection of articles in favor of revolution in France. It built on similar principles of Common Sense, renouncing the monarchial system of government as inhumane and self-serving with no upside for anyone outside the aristocracy. His ideas were founded on the rights of all people to include life, liberty, free speech, freedom of conscience. These were new ideas in Europe and word had spread of the success of the American Republic.

What made his arguments strong and persuasive was his consistent ability in written prose to blueprint a new society. He not only encouraged freedom, he demonstrated clear ideas about how to improve society through welfare programs designed to help the poor gain a foothold in life as independent people.

Age of Reason

Common Sense and Rights of Man extolled the argument for equality and liberty and denounced sovereignty. Age of Reason took these ideas and pressed on with popular Enlightenment Era themes that questioned institutionalized religion. It was not meant to disgrace faith, but to raise awareness about the politics of religion. Paine directed the masses' attention to the corruption that placed church and state at a level of power and governance over society. He pointed out the divine rights of the monarchy that essentially allowed them to be the head of the church as they existed in France with Louis XVI, and in England with King George as the head of the Church of England.

Why was this important? It was timely. The Enlightenment Era popularized free thought. It encouraged the average person to understand the ideas of liberty, equality and thinking for one's self. It rejected oppression. It empowered. Common sense, rights and reason were new ideas in the late 1700s. They were becoming subjects that people could actually discuss and debate in taverns and pubs.

Thomas Paine risked a lot to make these arguments available to the public and so did his publishers. He was charged with seditious libel in England and never returned to his country of birth, remaining in France. His legacy is an important one. Many scholars, both men and women, generated essays and articles from the ideals sparked in Thomas Paine's books. Although, England was not a place he could return to, Paine's blueprint for a welfare system in Rights of Man was something that found form later in England. He inspired a movement that ignited revolution for liberty and equality. This movement crossed oceans. The British colonies became the American Republic and Europe was marching into a new era of toppled sovereignty.

How is Thomas Paine relevant today? He was controversial and at the same time extremely influential. He wrote with logic infused with emotion that spoke to ordinary people. He was not concerned with filtering his thoughts for special interest groups. Paine challenged citizens to reject status quo and forge a new world that gave dignity to human beings and championed self-determination. His dogged determination to give voice to liberty and equality inspired throughout our history and is woven in our fabric through the abolition of slavery, suffrage, the Civil Rights Movement, freedom of choice and LGBTQ rights.

CHAPTER 14

Warp Speed Technology

For the last 15 years, social media has essentially created a world without borders. It has been a behavioral transformation phenomenon for any human on the planet with a smart phone or computer. What social media has confirmed is our need as human beings to explore, to share, to be curious and to stay connected to others.

A Short Story about a BIG "Book"

As 2005 came to a close, high schools, colleges and universities—populated with young Millennials—were unknowingly changing the world as we knew it through their introduction to Facebook. In 2006, Facebook became accessible to the rest of us and within one year went from 12 million members to 50 million members. Facebook Marketplace became the internet's new Craig's List, with far reaching potential to connect with friends—or friends of friends—or the entire world—your choice. Hundreds of thousands of businesses joined the Facebook frenzy to "get social" with their customers and friends of their customers and the entire world.

In 2010, Facebook reached 500 million in users and valued the company at $41 billion. When Instagram grabbed the social spotlight, Facebook took ownership of the IG world as well—for $1 billion. The influence and power of Facebook are extraordinary. It chronicles lives and takes us to faraway places. Facebook allows us to buy things from all over the world, connect via Messenger and Portal and share ideas. It is the probably the largest successful "social experiment" in the history of the world. Facebook has been instrumental in branding the largest generation, the Millennials, as collaborative change-makers. The social media giant hatched in a dorm room in Cambridge, Massachusetts, has spread across the world and changed human communication forever.

The Warp-Speed of Technology

Does anyone remember the Netscape vs. Microsoft browser war of the 1990s? Neither survived the browser clash, and by the early millennium Google was becoming a household name. Life before Wi-Fi is a distant memory, and the freedom that Wi-Fi created to connect without a cable anywhere a user can get a signal is a daily efficiency we take for granted.

Then came CGI (Computer Generated Imaging) changing the film industry with incredible graphics and the ability to tell epic stories involving a cast of thousands who were actually computer generated. Smart phones allow us to connect with anyone, anywhere, in a multitude of different media—through voice, video, text, and innovative apps.

Thanks to Google Earth we have a window on the world from the comfort of our homes via laptop or phone. Every human on the planet that has a smart phone and a signal can upload photos and videos of experiences and amazing places around the globe. It is a virtual travel, magic carpet ride in high definition. We are all sharing our lives from every corner of the globe with the rest of the world. The social network has broadened our horizons, our interests and it has raised awareness and increased activism. We are more connected not just to our local environment, but also the environment around the world.

Technology has changed the face of education and retail through virtual classroom and storefronts. Walking into a physical space to learn or shop is no longer routine. According to *Inside Higher Ed*, one-third of all enrolled students take an online class. An article posted by Fareeha Ali on *Digital Commerce 360* in March 2020 describes the eCommerce environment showing tremendous increases as 10 years ago online shopping represented "5.1% of total retail sales and now accounts for 16%. Consumers spent $601.75 billion online in the U.S. in 2019, a 14.9% jump compared with 2018." Most large U.S. mall-anchoring department stores are managing this shift in how consumers are making their purchases by either consolidating locations, or altering their interiors to accommodate online returns and to carry less in-house inventory. These numbers are likely much higher amidst the recent events of the COVID pandemic and will have lasting influence on university education.

Business, education and consumer spending can operate through software application. Instagram and Facebook have brought small retailers to the world marketplace with a scroll and a swipe. These retail platforms have provided opportunities to under-developed and developing countries with digital access to sell inexpensive goods globally.

Technology has made the world smaller and more inclusive. The ability for businesses to use crowd sourcing to attract and decipher information from a large group of participants has changed marketing and research and produced real data for growth and trends. Behavioral marketing is embedded into everything we view on our screens, serving us ads that serve our interests. We have amazing tech-savvy efficiencies that increase in scope and update daily, while a subtly accepted surveillance state has emerged cataloguing every human action and interaction flowing from our smart tech.

Precision Medicine

The American society has gone from the village doctor that made house calls to HMOs and PPOs, and most recently to virtual doctor's visits via smartphone. The rise of pharmaceuticals has innovated to save lives as well as created codependences that have destroyed lives. Our healthcare infrastructure is crippled with outrageous costs that have been a political hot button for decades, with no clear-cut solutions.

The new age of precision medicine is about to change how we manage our health care. Smart phones and watches can now perform real time vital sign checks, not only saving lives but conditioning us to understand how our bodies function under changing circumstances. Will a more informed patient make a healthier individual with less doctor's visits and preempted emergencies?

Precision prescriptions take on-demand real time patient vital statistics a step further by customizing dosing. For example, blood pressure, blood thinners, statin drugs, etc., would be reduced from potentially six pills into one "poly pill" that accommodates a patient's medical requirements based on their real time vital reading for the day. Will a consolidated version of a person's daily dose reduce prescription costs?

The promise of scientific advances in medicine that can replace mutated genes with healthy copies through gene therapy, and the phenomenal possibilities of 3-D organ printing, can someday become reality. When we achieve the ability to print viable 3-D organs, what happens next and how will we navigate the subset of issues and choices that surface from that technology?

The New Frontier of Artificial Intelligence

The efficiencies technology has brought to the daily activities of the human race are astounding. According to the OEDC (Organization for Economic Cooperation and Development) Americans work an average of 1,786 hours per year, above the average of OEDC member countries of 1,734 hours per year. Not surprisingly, American workers are known for longer working hours. But with all of our growing technology have the hours clocked diminished with greater efficiencies, or is our world so consumer driven that we are always trying to catch up with demand?

Artificial Intelligence introduces more than just technological efficiency. Does it put the human race at risk of no longer being *human*? There are great arguments for the need in certain industries to automate via AI to increase productivity, accuracy, safety and ultimately profitability. Manufacturing trucks responsible for getting goods around the globe could be well served with AI. Less potential for accidents, tired drivers, but what happens to the industry of drivers? Do they become obsolete, or do they remain onboard as the human copilot with the responsibility of overseeing the AI driver? Do we replace research analysts with AI data analysts to reduce human error and the monotony of collecting data in a bio lab or a law office? Rest assured technology will no longer be a utility working in the background.

What are the ramifications of Artificial Intelligence? When we introduce AI to handle data, outcomes and provide indefatigable precision in the workplace, as humans do we begin to lose relevance as we have known it, or does it become a shift in focus for our daily tasks?

Pew Research did a study on this subject, asking experts in the fields of technology, strategic thinking, scholars, practitioners and education leaders what they saw by "2030 ... for AI and related technology systems: will [they] enhance human capacities and empower them? ... will most people be better off than they are today? Or is it most likely that advancing AI and related technology systems will lessen human autonomy and agency to such an extent that most people will not be better off than the way things are today?"

Over 60% of the participants responded positively, seeing a future with AI as a benefit to people. However, there are some caveats that individuals and lawmakers need to keep at the forefront of this brave new world:

- **Sonia Katyal**, co-director of the Berkeley Center for Law and Technology and a member of the inaugural U.S. Commerce Department Digital Economy Board of Advisors, predicted, *"In 2030, the greatest set of questions will involve* *how perceptions of AI and their application will influence the trajectory of civil rights in the future. Questions about privacy, speech, the right of assembly and technological construction of personhood will all re-emerge in this new AI context, throwing into question our deepest-held beliefs about equality and opportunity for all. Who will benefit and who will be disadvantaged in this new world depends on how broadly we analyze these questions today, for the future."*

- **Michael M. Roberts**, first president and CEO of the Internet Corporation for Assigned Names and Numbers (ICANN) and Internet Hall of Fame member, wrote, *"The range of opportunities for intelligent agents to augment human intelligence is still virtually unlimited. The major issue is that the more convenient an agent is, the more it needs to know about you—preferences, timing, capacities, etc.—which creates a tradeoff of more help requires more intrusion. This is not a black-and-white issue—the shades of gray and associated remedies will be argued endlessly. The record to date is that convenience overwhelms privacy. I suspect that will continue."*

- **Greg Shannon**, Chief Scientist for the CERT Division at Carnegie Mellon University, said, *"Better/worse will appear 4:1 with the long-term ratio 2:1. AI will do well for repetitive work where 'close' will be good enough and humans dislike the work. … Life will definitely be better as AI extends lifetimes, from health apps that intelligently 'nudge' us to health, to warnings about impending heart/stroke events, to automated health care for the underserved (remote) and those who need* *extended care (elder care). As to liberty, there are clear risks. AI affects agency by creating entities with meaningful intellectual capabilities for monitoring, enforcing and even punishing individuals. Those who know how to use it will have immense potential power over those who don't/can't. Future happiness is really unclear. Some will cede their agency to AI in games, work and community, much like the opioid crisis steals agency today. On the other hand, many will be freed from mundane, unengaging tasks/jobs. If elements of community happiness are part of AI objective functions, then AI could catalyze an explosion of happiness."*

The onset of smart technology has produced many privacy concerns ranging from protecting sensitive personal or health information to unauthorized posting on social media. As smart tech has opened the window to freedom of speech, it has released privacy. Most of our younger population has grown up with smart technology and AI from a very young age. They trust it implicitly. It has created more efficiency and convenience in their lives than they even realize.

Has anyone seen a Gen Z try to use a phone book or a rotary desk phone? Regardless of age, we all are used to electronic technologies. They make our lives easier.

The flip side is they gather information from the user 24/7. As many times as we Ask Siri or Alexa for information, these smart technologies are recording our habits, visits and keystrokes. The data matrix is apparently infinite and it travels all over the globe as easily as we travel on Instagram or Google Earth.

It's something to consider, isn't it? Change is constant. Have we arrived at a point of techno bliss and convenience that is blind to historical repeat?

CHAPTER 15

Our History, Our Future Revealed in the Present Moment

According to an article published in the New England Journal of Medicine, January 19, 2020, will become a date that should be of great significance historically, as it marks the first case of confirmed COVID-19 in the U.S. Many of us watched and read about reports a hemisphere away as Wuhan, China, grappled with the overwhelming contagion of this virus. When the virus hit U.S. soil and rapidly spread amongst a population in Washington State, Americans watched and waited as cases of COVID-19 began to rapidly multiply across the map. By Easter weekend, well over 500,000 Americans were diagnosed with Coronavirus and the U.S. death toll from the virus was over 22,000.

This tragedy of a highly contagious global virus was something all of humanity shared. It did not discriminate. We watched in disbelief as this virus decimated populations in Italy, whose general population is so much smaller than China or the U.S. By mid-March, COVID-19 was present in all 50 U.S. States. We had closed our borders and declared a national state of emergency.

By mid-April, most of the country had followed suit. We were an eerily quiet nation with minimal air, freeway and street traffic. Our education systems closed their doors and continued their semesters virtually. WFH became the "new normal." Sports networks ran reruns of seasons gone by. Parks and beaches were closed. Nature became so visceral, as it was the only living process that did not alter its day to day.

Adversity Exposes the True Measure of People and Society

One of the tenets of the New Thought philosophy is the Law of Attraction, the belief that positive or negative thoughts and deeds, bring positive or negative experiences into a person's life. Human history bears witness to moments and events that show the harmony, as well as the chaos of this philosophy at work.

We closed our borders and we got to work, as Americans do, in the face of crisis. This was the first time a national emergency had occurred since 9/11 and almost 20 years later Americans rallied together to show resilience, commitment and how much we value protecting our society when faced with life changing events. We have worked together against a common enemy in a deep and rich way that will have lasting benefits for our communities and society.

This pandemic challenge has tested our common humanity and our vulnerability. What has mattered during this troubled time is the smile we put on people's faces who are shut in by doing a virtual call or a drive-by visit or how we honor and support our first responders on the front lines of this crisis. Or how we reconnect with our families as we WFH and finish the school year virtually from our kitchen tables.

The first responders and essential workers have demonstrated tireless commitment to caring for the sick, saving lives and providing the services necessary for daily needs. Their badges of honor are the facial lines created from a full day, 24 hours or more, in face masks and protective gear. The commitment to our communities and country with the flexibility shown by business and industry who have redirected their manufacturing focus from cars to ventilators, from alcohol distilleries to hand sanitizer manufacturing and from baseball uniforms to hospital gowns and masks. As families, we have moved from busy lives full of activities and consumption to a more meditative approach to our days as we navigate a new conservancy, eat home cooked meals and adjust to a new concept of time.

We have witnessed "sideline heroes" who put forth their personal time to volunteer to shop for elderly people whose health risk is too great to venture out in public; scenes of people with piles of unused fabric scraps who have dusted off their sewing machines to make masks for the community; the many support groups that knew their members needed meetings to continue their paths of recovery and set up virtual meetings to keep their members healthy and connected. These are the feel-good stories and the positivity of the law of attraction that encourages humanity to come together and generate the processes that prop up society.

Adversity Exposes the True Measure of Politicians and the News Media

This is where our society falls short and the people who are most visible on a continual basis are at fault. There has been a lot of criticism on border closings—how do you mitigate a pandemic without closing borders and restricting travel for a period of time? It is COMMON SENSE. What is truly disturbing during these difficult times is the consistent inability for representatives to put politics aside and focus on solving the problems that the pandemic has brought to our society and our economy.

It is completely disgraceful and meaningless that the news media and our U.S. representatives continue to propagate divisive banter. Why is any elected representative putting forth requests that represent an agenda that does not speak to the immediacy of the economic fallout of the pandemic? The creation of the stimulus package is designed to help Americans keep the lights on, a roof over their heads and food on the table. Stimulus was designed to keep our economy running so we have jobs to return to and companies can survive. It was designed to keep our hospitals and caregivers fully supplied to care for the overload of patients affected by the pandemic.

Politicians and the news media who are trying to attract voters and viewership with negativity and fear are imploding. They have incorrectly calculated American "buy in" to their brand of party power. They have assumed the role of behavioral marketers in the hopes that they can easily prey on reactivity with the emotions of fear and anger, rather than reason and intellect.

The most vital questions to issues and events that beg investigation are becoming taboo, inappropriate or conspiracy theory fodder. Where is the groundbreaking investigative journalism? Where have the U.S. Representatives gone who are supposed to be sitting in Washington voting on American issues and allow proxy *in absentia*? What has happened is that these two entities have alienated American society. The news media have embraced subjects of conflict within the 24/7 news cycle to compete with other news outlets. Politicians have used this news cycle to disparage each other. No one wins and Americans sit on the sidelines frustrated. It has led to distrust and a society left unfulfilled by the information and lack of edification the news media provides, as well as a lack of solidarity with elected officials leading together.

Veiling America

In June 2020 wearing a mask became mandatory in the State of Virginia. This is a practice we may not shed for a very long time. We have been viewing the Asian population donning masks for years and perhaps longer than we realize. Japanese, Chinese and Korean cultures have been covering mouths and noses since the time of the 1918 Spanish Flu that infected the entire world. There lies one of the inherent dangers of large populations. Population is staggering in some of the cities of these Asian countries, with Tokyo topping the list at over 37 million people. Delhi, Shanghai, Dhaka, Mumbai, Beijing and Osaka are all in the top ten most populated cities in the world.

The mask served the purpose of not just guarding against communicable disease, but also protection from smog and carbon dioxide.

China's tremendous export market puts their country at the top of the list of most polluted countries in the world. There is another piece to this practice as well: Asian cultures are influenced by the practice of Taoism and the Eastern Medicine precept of "Qi," breathing and breath as essential to good health. April 2020 saw a huge response from the fashion industry in the U.S. with couture mask-wear. Hundreds of home industry seamstresses have gone to work utilizing fabric remnants for colorful masks. The mask may become *de rigueur* as social distancing creates new rules within safety and etiquette. We are a country built on liberties and individuality. We are expressive. It has proven difficult for Americans to cover up as it seems counterintuitive to freedoms. Unfortunately, reluctant mask wearers have shown that their short-sightedness has encouraged the virus to linger and grow in the U.S. If the uptick in COVID cases settles in throughout the country, mask wearing may very well be here to stay, as we ebb and flow through the pandemic's lifespan.

Will the friendly handshake begin to disappear as the commitment to limit physical contact takes hold of our daily interactions? Perhaps Americans will adopt the Eastern hemisphere's tradition of the bowed head in reverence when greeting people socially rather than risk potential transmission. Again, this may be tough for Americans—we like to "bring it in"; we appreciate the human connection that a hug brings. It is one of the ways we enjoy the freedom to love and appreciate each other.

The Opportunities that Lie in Adversity

There have been good news stories all over social media regarding the impact social distancing has had on the environment. A substantial decrease in air, road and water traffic has reduced the amount of emissions in hot spots around the world. While we do need to understand that that only lasts as long as the Earth is experiencing the traffic hiatus brought on by a global pandemic, it does offer humanity a glimpse at the immediate significance of changing habits on a global scale. We can see the difference. When COVID-19 slows to a trickle, we will be business as usual and ramp up our travel and our emissions, but the opportunity IS there to see the impact that changes in routine, changes in travel and changes in dealing with our waste can produce meaningful change in our environment.

Technology drives everyday life in American society. Imagine life during the 1918 Spanish Flu. We did not have the laboratory technology to bring drug remedy and vaccines to the marketplace and far more lives were lost. The Spanish Flu took an estimated 50 million lives. As devastating as COVID-19 has been, we are so fortunate to live in a time that has the technology to abate the contagion to a far greater degree. By late July 2020 worldwide deaths were close to 650,000 with approximately 145,000 of those deaths occurring in the U.S. Technology and easy access to information have allowed the general public to be educated and updated on the nature of the virus, how to mitigate the spread and safety. Technology has given us the opportunity to spend time virtually with our families and friends while social distancing. So many businesses have been extremely hard hit by the virus, but many have been able to sustain through Work from Home, online shopping, takeout and delivery.

The reality is the economy will take some time to recover. Americans will not go back to the same life we had prior to COVID-19. Not necessarily a bad thing. There are always opportunities in adversity. It is all about strategy, attitude and learning from previous experiences. We will not walk away unscathed, but we will rebuild and our society may become better for the experience. The hold on the economy has given many of us pause to reevaluate what is important in life. We have fast-forwarded to a "tipping point" in life with a need for a reset.

Whether it has been the realization to move on from a job, a relationship that was unhealthy or reengaging in family life, there will be change going forward. We will certainly have new protocols to adjust to, just as we did after 9/11. Our dependence on exports from China may change. Businesses may have lower profit margins if that occurs, but Americans are innovators and that will be a challenge that we are sure to overcome. Maybe Artificial Intelligence is the answer to the challenge of manufacturing goods in high demand, with unlimited supply for less cost. Just as Americans came to the realization we were not dependent on the Middle East for oil, we may very well find we do not depend on China for cheaper goods in the future.

COVID-19 has, and will continue to impact the legal system in the U.S. and globally for years to come. Will the backlogged court system present an opportunity for judicial reforms?

The Novel Coronavirus has brought tragedy and grave challenges, but it has also created reconnection and collaboration and it has brought us heroes, innovation and a sense of community back to the American culture.

The Eight Minutes and Forty-Six Seconds that Redirected the Conversation

"I can't breathe…" An African American man lay face down and pinned at the neck between a car tire and the knee of a white police officer whose full weight crushed George Floyd's airway. The man was on the ground; his hands were cuffed behind his back. There were three police officers on him. He was able to gasp out the words several times that he "Could … Not … Breathe." The officers were unrelenting.

His crime was passing a counterfeit $20 bill at a convenience store to buy cigarettes. My husband (white male) could have easily walked into any establishment not knowing he had counterfeit currency in his wallet and passed it innocently through a purchase—or, he could have passed it knowingly. Regardless, does anyone really think that justice would have placed a white male cuffed, face down and pinned at the neck until he could no longer breathe for the exact same crime?

In a 2019 Pew Research Center study: "84% of black adults said that, in dealing with police, blacks are generally treated less fairly than whites; 63% of whites said the same. Similarly, 87% of blacks and 61% of whites said the U.S. criminal justice system treats black people less fairly."

In exploring racial inequality and police brutality, I want to be very clear that I value law and order. I think most people do. I have a family member who has over a twenty-year career in law enforcement. He is a fair and responsible law enforcement officer. He is a keen observer of the human condition, respects human life and human dignity. He is an incredible man and someone I consider a role model. He does not abuse the power he has been given. Law enforcement dedicate their lives to protecting the community; they are potentially put in harm's way every day and officers who dispatch equitable and humane law enforcement deserve our respect.

That said, the other systemic problem we face occurs when there are bad actors within law enforcement or government who abuse the power they have been given to serve and protect. There is a massive racial confidence gap in police performance. We witness episodes of misconduct, racial injustice and violent repression of the First Amendment.

In a recent TED Talks Daily podcast episode, Dr. Phillip Atiba Goff, the founder and CEO of the Center for Policing Equity, joined other guests to discuss the racial divide and the path to ending systemic racism in the U.S. Dr. Goff's work is with police departments around the country—including Minneapolis—to achieve measurable responses to racial bias. His treatment of the issue, his eloquence in giving voice to understanding the path to resolution and how as a culture we have consistently derailed ourselves from committing to that path, is extraordinary as it is heartbreaking:

> . . . this week has been a gut punch to anybody who felt like we could be making progress in the way that we put forward public safety that empowers particularly vulnerable communities. We started working in Minneapolis about five years ago. At the time, it was, like most major cities in the United

States, a department that had a long history of unaccounted for violence from law enforcement, targeting the most vulnerable black communities. And we tried to put into place a number of things that we know work.

Change the culture so that the culture can be accountable to the values of the community. And what we saw was small but measurable progress. We always knew, with small and measurable progress, that you're one tragic incident from going back to ground zero.

But the events of the last week and a half haven't brought us back to ground zero, they've torched ground zero, and we've dug a hole that we have to dig ourselves out of. What I hear from police chiefs who call me, from activists I talk to, from folks in the communities that are literally on fire right now...I had one activist say to me that the pain that he was feeling was too large to fit into his body.

And without thinking about it, I said right back, "That's because it's too large to fit into a lifetime."

What we're seeing isn't just the response to one gruesome, cruel, public execution. A lynching. It's not just the reaction to three of them: Ahmaud Arbery, Breonna Taylor and then George Floyd. What we're seeing is the bill come due for the unpaid debts that this country owes to its black residents. And it comes due usually every 20 to 30 years.

It was Ferguson just six years ago, but about 30 years before that, it was in the streets of Los Angeles, after the verdict that exonerated the police that beat Rodney King on video. It was Newark, it was Watts, it was Chicago, it was Tulsa, it was Chicago again. If we don't take a full accounting of these debts that are owed, then we're going to keep paying it.

... the soul-crushing reality [is] that at some point, when things stop being on fire, the cameras are going to turn to something else. And the history that we have in this country is not just a history of vicious neglect and a targeted abuse of black communities, it's also one where we lose our attention for it. And what that means for communities like in Baton Rouge, for those who still grieve Alton Sterling, and in Baltimore, for those who are still grieving Freddie Gray ...there's a likelihood that we are a month or two months out from this with no more to show for it than what we had to show after Michael Brown, Jr. And holding the weight of that, individually and collectively, is just too much. It's just too heavy a load for a person or a people, or a generation to hold up.

What we're seeing is the unrepentant sins, the unpaid debts. And so the solution can't just be that we fix policing. It can't be only incremental reform. It can't be only systems of account-ability to catch cops after they've killed somebody. Because there's no such thing as justice for George Floyd. There's maybe accountability. There's maybe some relief from the people who are still around, who loved him, for his daughter who spoke out yesterday and said, "My Daddy changed the world." There won't be justice for a man who's dead when he didn't have to be. But we're not going to get to where we need to go just by reforming police.

Our news cycle has created a world of "social acceleration" that allows the negativity of presentism and invites cultural bias. We sift through as much information as our brains can effectively process, and that is the inherent problem with the 24-hour news cycle. Human brains cannot give collective attention to all of the information that flows through 24 hours. Our attention span narrows. We move on, and if we are not holding each other accountable as human beings then we will never change. Dr. Goff's words are extremely compelling. Simply changing one process that involves bad actors does not fix this. Dr. Phillip Goff is an African American man who has worked peacefully and intelligently to change the mentality that exists in an entity that can wield brutal and violent power over the individual. This is not just limited to police violence, and I am not suggesting that police reform is not of paramount importance. There are bad actors perpetuating racial bias, and injustice, in all walks of life—with examples reaching bank loan discrimination, neighborhood discrimination and employer discrimination.

Unpaid debts should not be the cue for lawyers to get rich collecting financial reparations for a history of injustice. That does not change a culture; it allows the almighty dollar to become of greater value than human dignity.

Unpaid debts are best paid when a society changes its attitudes on diversity, values human life and encourages individuals to be their best selves. That can be difficult to do when there is not a level playing field. Change the culture, change the conversation. These are freedoms philosophers waxed poetic about in the salons of Enlightenment Era Europe—give human beings equality and the opportunity to author their own soul. The young American republic took European philosophy and made it a reality—of sorts—it was a start. What we can learn from our young republic's history is that change began with a bottom up approach, a voice of powerful change among citizens with reason and purpose for how to achieve change. Our country's great beginnings were not a top down approach that involved upper layers of legislators, more government and ineffectual programs.

My hope is there are some uncomfortable readers right now. My hope is there is some acceptance and shame that this is a dark truth we struggle with in the land of freedom and equality. We are very capable of creating a united America during periods of national trauma, but systemic racism in this country remains a fixed liability that Americans have never addressed to work to the solution that changes the culture.

If They Can Erase Your Past, They Can Control Your Future

Around the time of the 25-year anniversary of Tiananmen Square—June 3, 2014—*Vox* did an article on the historical event. The article references Louisa Lim's book, <u>The People's Republic of Amnesia: Tiananmen Revisited.</u> There are interesting statistics that record the

Chinese government's official death toll from Tiananmen at 241 people. The estimates just within Beijing from eyewitnesses and the Red Cross are 2,600 to 2,700 fatalities.

A retrospective piece usually captures how people were feeling during that time, what they experienced and how the event has changed society 25 years later. Ms. Lim interviewed 100 students from prestigious Beijing universities. These students are extremely intelligent, well-travelled internationally, internet-savvy and evidently have what would be considered unusual in China, access to foreign media. They are sophisticated. Lim showed these students the photo that came to define the 1989 uprising of the young Chinese student standing in front of a military tank. Only 15 of the 100 were able to identify the photo as a symbol of Tiananmen Square.

A collective amnesia campaign initiated immediately by the Chinese government in 1989 declared Tiananmen a non-event. Other writers including the author of the Vox article experienced similar encounters with Chinese friends who had moved to the U.S. and recounted the event just as the Chinese government censored the massacre to reflect an unfortunate uprising of a small group of activists that was quietly and efficiently quelled. It is a real-life example of the Parable of Truth and Story. What is so astounding is that they have been successful in controlling the crafted story of the Tiananmen Massacre for a population of almost 1.4 billion people. They rewrote history.

Last spring my husband and I were in Berlin, and we met with a sharp 30-something Berliner named Dennis who taught at Potsdam University. We spent many hours with him, walking through the streets of Berlin as he took us through Berlin's terrible history under Nazi rule, and then Communist rule. Germany has handled an evil history a little differently than China.

Both of Dennis' grandfathers served as soldiers in Hitler's army. Dennis' generation was one that asked questions. He asked his grandfathers if they knew the depths of human rights violations and murder. The innocence of children asking questions to understand how this could happen, as loving adults struggled with the shameful answer. It is an evil heritage Dennis owns stoically as his ancestors' horrific past, as he in turn describes the way in which Germans since 1945 have worked to atone for it.

It is almost impossible to walk any street in Berlin without encountering a brass plaque, a "stumbling stone" memorializing a murdered Jew. It is extremely sobering. Three generations of German school age children have learned to accept the terrible truth of their homeland's history. They have it drilled into their history lessons from primary school to high school and carry the burden of shame for the actions of their ancestors. We found it remarkable how German society committed to this level of atonement. They told the truth; they did not rewrite textbooks and they changed the culture.

There are dark truths in American history that perpetuate today, that we cannot forget. That we must own. Removing American Confederate statues that venerate a society that refused to change their culture of subjugation and slavery is long overdue. The removal of these statues from our public spaces is only a gesture if we are not committing to a cultural reawakening. It is only a gesture if groups bent on creating chaos continue to indiscriminately include statues in the "statue leveling movement" that bear no significance to the cause. They only become a device to enlist anarchy and increase the divide and polarization.

It would be interesting to offer a challenge to the "statue leveling movement" to articulate and educate us all on the meaning behind the destruction of the Ulysses S. Grant statue in San Francisco. Grant led the Union Army in the fight to end slavery. I would like to understand the strategy behind destroying the statue honoring black revolutionary soldiers in Boston. Perhaps there is an explanation regarding the statue of Frederick Douglass, the renowned Abolitionist, torn from its pedestal in Rochester, New York.

> *"Do the best you can until you know better. Then when you know better, do better."*—**Maya Angelou**

Americans have created a culture over the last 350+ years through some trial, some triumph and a lot of status quo in its quest to defend freedom and dignity. We take small steps of victory to change the way we think, how we act and how we treat each other. Then we forget our best selves, and we allow the darkness of human nature to guide our thinking and we lose sight of something as simple as "The Golden Rule." We allow polarization to win.

COVID-19 has revealed poignant glimpses of the best in humanity, and then the culmination of the murders of Ahmaud Arbery, Breonna Taylor and then George Floyd exposed the dark truth of American democracy. Just like that, we reversed progress measured in miles, not steps.

Will the contrast of these major events of 2020, the dawn of a new decade, and the greatest American diversity to date—in the Millennial generation—bring us back to the importance of the human race and upend the status quo? Will this generation be the needed catalyst to change what is so desperately void within our American culture of democracy? Real change. Real transparency. Real conversations. Real equality. This dawning of a new decade is the opening act for the "big reveal" for our American future.

CHAPTER 16

The *[New]* New Patriotism

Change is constant. Throughout history human beings have shown that while we do not always prepare for change, we have the ability to adapt rapidly to change in motion. We wind through centuries and eras without fully realizing we have just crossed over to another time. We find ourselves at another place in history with different approaches, priorities and desires for what makes a society great, what makes it thrive and what makes it endure.

One of the most interesting challenges for 2020, and the new decade, will be an America that can retain its essence while living in a globally accessible environment. It is the challenge for most countries with a strong historical patriotism. Look at the rise of Populism in the U.S. and countries around the world. Watching this happen collectively across the globe is a strong signal that countries are feeling that they are losing their cultural identity and are looking for leadership that will preserve and grow it. As we become a more global society, we are no longer as exotic, yet we still want to retain the core of what makes our cultures unique.

The Rise of Isolationism and Decline of Trust

9/11 changed life in the U.S. and around the world as Americans embarked on a new collaboration with world allies while simultaneously becoming more isolationist. Our First Responders became our heroes for months on end as they continued to clear away the rubble and the thousands of lost lives from the Towers, the Pentagon and the field in Somerset County, PA. We joined the ranks of Europe and the Middle East's more recent histories, as our nation was rocked by the unconscionable acts of terrorism.

American patriotism was awakened from a long slumber. Our society was shaken and our homeland safety was found extremely vulnerable. We gathered together to overcome the tragedy and to come to the aid of those whose lives were forever changed by that September day. This was a defining moment for Americans. The U.S. entered into a retaliatory war and continued conflict with Iraq and Afghanistan that has lasted for almost 20 years. Tolerance for the Iraq War is vastly different from its Vietnam predecessor of 50 years prior. The horrific events of 9/11 placed most Americans squarely on the side of defending our country by show of force. Unlike Vietnam, the Iraq War and continued conflict did not involve the requirement of a military draft.

With a war fought 50 years after Vietnam, the ability for the American military to "conduct" a war, technologically via drones, has vastly changed the level of human involvement and resulting casualties. Americans had more of a stomach for the Iraq War, and with far less casualties and no draft. The Iraq War droned on for years with a certain public apathy. Vietnam held far more emotional trigger for a young generation unwilling to be forced by draft to serve.

9/11 increased Americans' distrust, with racial and ethnic profiling targeting those in our communities along with the practice of isolationism. It is an unfortunate byproduct of the event. There are examples in American communities where trying to be politically correct cost a missed opportunity to prevent additional acts of terrorism. There are also many examples of persecuting innocent groups of people who are trying to live their religion of choice in a country built on freedoms. Travel protocols became more complex to address illegal border crossings by persons of interest. Homeland vigilance is an inexact science. We have made mistakes.

Young Millennials during this time watched their Baby Boomer parents live this history and ironically, Millennial adults are more diverse and are a more accepting generation than their parents. They are curious about the world and the people who inhabit it. The world is an infinite social experiment in the eyes of the Millennials—with no limits.

Diversity Matters

Statistics reveal the shift in racial demographics of the Boomer generation in relation to the Millennial generation. Some key demographic statistics taken from the 2010 U.S. Census reveal the following evolution of racial diversity among Baby Boomers versus Millennials: Within the total 2010 U.S. Census population, 26% of the Baby Boomer generation identified as White, 20% as African American, 20% as Native American, 19% as Asian, 13% as Hispanic and 2% as Other. Contrast those demographics with the younger Millennial generation against the total U.S. Census population and the same study found 16% of the Millennial generation identified as White, 18% as Asian, 18% as Native Hawaiian/Pacific Islander, 17% as Hispanic, 16% as African American, 15% as Native American.

The numbers show real change in what the next generation looks like in terms of race. Americans are a society of increasing diversity; perhaps for the first time since Ellis Island of our immigrant ancestors, and the Millennial generation is almost evenly distributed among race classifications. Additionally, in a Pew Research study almost 92% LGBT Americans felt society was more accepting of their sexual orientation than they had the decade prior. In June 2015 the Supreme Court struck down State bans on same sex marriages. Those groups who felt previously disenfranchised now have a more firm voice in society.

The New Patriotism—20 Years in the Making

The Millennial Generation of change is strong; they are the largest generation population in American history. Diversity is key in this currently 25–40-year-old generation, but so are the level of higher education and the rising age of marriage. Pew Research Center's data indicate that 39% percent of Millennials have completed a bachelor's degree or higher compared to their parents' Boomer generation of about 25%. Another noticeable education shift is in the percentage of Millennial women out pacing men in college degrees, with 43% of the women completing undergraduate education versus 36% of the men.

Between the ages of 25–37 only 46% of Millennials are married, during the same age range the Boomer generation was about 67% married. What this data may indicate is a shift that has most likely been influenced by empowered young women finding career advancement opportunities taking precedence over marital commitment.

Millennials are swift on change as technology has not only facilitated efficiencies in work and personal lives, but also in how we interact and collaborate in those spheres as well. Facebook, SnapChat, Airbnb, Instagram, the Honest Company, Pinterest, Lyft and WordPress are just a few of the Millennial-founded companies that have created monumental societal impact. They have forged the "experience economy" as well as defined a new personal and corporate accountability that strives for transparency, environmental priority while encouraging a self-expression that has further defined the American way of life. Companies such as Lyft, Airbnb, Booking.com, and Trip Advisor have taken the shift away from a corporate reliance on spending and offered inventive ways of enjoying a quality of life with self-expression and entrepreneurship. The mentality has become more "win-win" for the consumer, the entrepreneur and the corporation.

By the way, that's exactly the priority sequence Millennials want to see the win taking place. They champion the individual and demand transparency from big business.

What's happened as a result is that traditional corporations such as Marriott are taking notice and offering new product lines that cater to the individually tailored "experience economy." Millennials are bringing back and redefining American cultural freedoms with greater diversity, defined experiences and with greater influence. However, a red flag should be raised on how these expressive freedoms are being hijacked by the back channels of technology.

Aeternae Libertatis

Eternal liberty should find itself entrenched in the American lexicon, rather than endangered by division and chaos. American culture has been built on freedom and civil liberties. The Millennial generation is more inclusive than prior generations and they seek global collaboration. Against the rise of populism, the recent increase of xenophobia in the U.S. and in Europe speaks to a loud minority that would like to revert to a mentality that has been abandoned by the 21st century. This minority is vocal and place themselves in environments where they can promote racial bias. There is a clash of human wills that rather than courageously propel a society forward uses intimidation and hate because they are afraid of what lies beyond a new horizon.

Accepting racial diversity and equality is not the only issue threatening civil liberties and sustaining a future for the American society and clearing the path for a new definition of the American patriot. Unlimited information access has taught us empowerment. We have infinite possibilities to gather information.

We have infinite educational resources. From something as simple as watching a DIY YouTube video to taking online classes toward a degree, these technology efficiencies no longer confine an individual to a bricks and mortar classroom, or the financial handcuffs of exorbitant tuition. Our high tech lives have inspired a new generation to think completely out of the box and the Millennials are here to teach us all, whether you are American or not; that change is here. Whatever your technology fantasies are, they will likely come to fruition in our lifetimes.

Our reliance on smart technology is a Pandora's Box of information for the consumer. The quest for knowledge online becomes an open gift, and technology can be the ultimate giver. As with all cautionary tales involving human nature, we are often caught off guard by the downside of the technology "woo." Totalitarianism is masked in technology swag when tech asks for information in return for what it offers the consumer. Smart tech's guiles are far more subtle when it is able to gather information without the consumer's tacit consent through GPS, allowing technology to monitor an individual's whereabouts virtually 24/7.

Technology has wrapped us in its arms and swaddled us. Empowerment is a powerful tool. However, the efficiencies that technology creates can enable humans to move through life without honing certain skills. What happens to problem solving if the answer is always a click away? What happens to reading body language and assessing the person you are interacting with if you are engaging with one another via text or video chat? Does it change and potentially evolve the nature of discourse and negotiation? These are skill sets that are powerful human tools required for diplomacy in personal, work life and government interactions. These are skills that require continuous refining so that we as humans can support our instincts.

One of the most important tenets to staying true to the American values of freedom is maintaining an open and transparent society.

The importance of understanding the ramifications of technology, artificial intelligence and central surveillance are huge. In 2018, two separate articles were published in The Atlantic and Business Insider that forewarned of the impending "Social Credit System" in China, a monitoring system that by 2020, will track the moves of every citizen of China's extremely large populations, including law infractions and postings of dissent on social media outlets and resulting in a "score" that will impact their ability to find employment commensurate with their skill level, with the cascade effect of determining what housing and education status their families can benefit from.

We should be asking ourselves how our civil liberties are compromised—these vital core values of American patrimony—if we live in an increasingly surveilled nation via subverted technology. This is a question that belongs in every American conversation. Against the riptide of technology, what will the new American value system of civil liberties look like? China is transparent in announcing to its citizens that they are surveilled, judged and merited on the basis of their behaviors and conformity. American techno surveillance is not so transparent.

Unprecedented Times

COVID-19 reengaged some of the emotional moments of 20 years ago. By mid-May 2020, approximately 80,000 Americans and over 280,000 people globally had perished from an extremely contagious global virus and an invisible enemy. The COVID-19 pandemic has illustrated the globalization of society while exposing the intrinsic nature of every society to isolate and defend in times of conflict.

What makes this event different is that the Millennial generation is now fully adult, spanning from 25–40 years old. Their parents are the age group at greatest risk during the pandemic and they are raising young children amidst these challenges. The "sandwich generation" torch has passed to the Millennials. This pandemic has reinforced this issue of national security in a new way. 9/11 closed borders and travel for a period of time. COVID-19 has far exceeded that by shutting down the country to travel and business for over two months. The result has been catastrophic, not just in terms of lives lost, but in crippling a U.S. economy that just two months prior was benefiting from the greatest economy in its history. Once again new protocols in safety are becoming centralized. For COVID-19, it will take 9/11's protocols a step further into health care, restaurants and public spaces, altering the American way of life.

Changing the Conversation for the New American Patriot

There are challenges this brave new face of American patriotism will encounter. COVID-19 has thrown a fly in the soup of the global community that exists today on the ease of travel and the accessibility of once "exotic" goods and services. There will be mitigation and this will be a challenge for a generational culture of global diversity.

We have struggled with systemic racism for centuries. There is hope and there are efforts within this generation that suggest Americans may finally move in the direction that represents real democracy. The Millennial generation has the unique distinction of being the first

American generation in history with an almost equal percentage of the population spread across race. It is the beginning of the removal of the word minority.

Millennials have taught us to "change the conversation, change the narrative." CHANGE. Learn how to have a conversation and it will change how people interact with one another. RESPECT. I APPRECIATE YOU. These words of kindness and gratitude are slowly finding their way back into the conversation. In the words of Stephen Covey, "Most people don't listen with the intent to understand, they listen with the intent to reply." Enter every conversation assuming you have something to learn and watch what happens: a culture open to acceptance and change rather than polarized by fear, anger and ignorance.

This Brave New World, This *New* New Patriotism

The last 20 years have changed the shape of American patriotism while the last ten have defined its course immeasurably. It becomes more than a beating drum for change. A new American patriotism becomes a fight for the soul of the nation. It becomes the realization that the American society—the civilization built on civil liberties—only survives time and the clash of human will if the culture is willing to change. The new American patriots are the change-makers of the culture.

If the Millennial generation is the largest stakeholder, American patriotism is most likely in the best hands since the Greatest Generation of the early 1900s. What makes Millennials so well prepared to handle change?

They prepare for it and, in their own words, they "curate" change. They are genuine in their collaboration efforts. Millennials have fostered a tremendously collaborative environment in all aspects of the lives they are building socially, personally, professionally and politically. They seek feedback constantly from a wide demographic. They invented the information junkie, the foodie, the bio hacker, the capsule wardrobe and virtual travel. Millennials reinvented lifestyle branding. This generation is brilliant at honing wants into needs.

This new American patriot is so self-expressive, collaborative and technologically advanced, they are masters of strategy and planning. They know how to gather information and develop metrics that determine outcomes. They know how to get results. Combine that with the fact that they were raised to be empowered, Millennials are extremely confident decision-makers and directors of protocol.

Social Consciousness

Because they have grown up with so many avenues of technology and conflicting accounts of information, they are also skeptical and ethical. They call out fake news. Social consciousness is front and center in all aspects of life. Millennials pay far more attention to how and where businesses spend their money, how they contribute to society, and the ethics behind the curtain of a company's "sales floor."

Economy

While Millennials have redefined much of how we live, they will absolutely benefit from revisiting historical perspective. They might want to revisit Milton Friedman, the brilliant economist, and his essays and speeches during the economic inflation of the 1970s. We are currently positioning for an economic reset as our country goes into greater debt to provide financial assistance to Americans during an unprecedented pandemic, while we continue to bail out European countries from a World War that happened over 80 years ago. That is an enormous burden Americans cannot afford.

They will want to revisit the war effort of the 1940s to understand that while Americans lived in a different time the challenges to defend and rebuild the country where not determined by well-dressed legislators voting on multi-trillion–dollar stimulus packages. Americans rolled up their sleeves, enlisted in the military, worked factory jobs and bought war bonds to help support the government. Not the reverse.

Politics

COVID-19 has a unique place in local government, the success stories and the failures. It will be interesting to see how this plays out for the long game, as demand for the autonomy of localized government may very well play a larger role than ever before. National politics have held the spotlight for over 150 years of American history. However, the divisive nature of a two-party system has worn thin with constituents who find their elected representatives more interested in planning coups rather than enacting positive and tangible societal improvements. Politicians are forgetting the People's business, and instead focusing major efforts and taxpayer dollars on destroying each other. In the next ten years, the new American patriot may very well create multiple political parties to disband partisan politics and bring more diverse idea groups to the table. After all, the Millennials are the great collaborators and change-makers.

The sacrifices our Founders made for a free country were on the scale none of us can envision in the American life we live today. Their success was incredibly unlikely and failure a probable outcome. In regard to collaboration, consider the partnerships necessary to create the documents that bind American patrimony—our heritage: The Declaration of Independence, the Federalist Papers, the U.S. Constitution, the Bill of Rights and Amendments. Our Founders were the original change-makers. While enacting change, understand the principles of these collaborated documents and safeguard their future in American society and government.

Human Rights and the Loss of Democracy Abroad

As we have embraced an American patriotism that is about defending our rights as much as defending the rights of others, this large generation will undoubtedly continue this charge as socially conscious humans. Democracy under the new American patriotism continues to be more than the dream that only happens in America. Millennials will brand that American model for democracy to other countries, and convey this message with deft ability. Their own diversity and yen for unique and authentic experiences will likely not compromise the essence of a country's culture. Rather they will encourage democracy to exist globally without losing diversity.

The great challenge this generation will face is how they will work with China, or not. Transparency at home while securing democracy and human rights abroad will play into intrepid decisions that will define the coming decades. China will be this generation's call to action:

- The human rights violations of the internment camps and the sterilization of Muslims in China is of great international concern.

- The systematic build-up in the South China Sea and international waterway disputes that threaten the world's largest trade route.

- The taking of free-market Hong Kong. Will Taiwan be the next "low hanging fruit?"

- The violent border conflicts with India—a democracy with the second largest population in the world next to China.

These are significant and strategic moves that have occurred in a very short period of time. China is the world's largest populated country with a totalitarian Communist government and a world superpower.

Civil Liberties

Exercise caution as you tread the global landscape, dear Millennials and your incumbent Gen Zs, because the technology that has given you the world in the palm of your hand has consequences. We are all enamored with the benefits of tech, but as you fiercely protect our democracy and champion transparency, keep watch of the surveillance that exists within technology. Facial recognition is a great example of the advances in recent technology. In terms of privacy and personal freedom—you can always leave your phone at home, but you cannot leave your face at home. How does that affect law abiding privacy? This is a civil liberties issue.

FOMO—Fear of Missing Out—has fed the news and information cycle to the extent that we discard information just as quickly as the new information arrives to replace it. Be present, but don't forget history or try to erase it. It is there for a reason. Do not allow fear and anger to lay waste to solving our cultural issues with reason and inclusivity. The Millennial generation has taken the politically correct language of decades ago that overcorrected the way we communicate to a more centered *be kind* to people. Show respect. This is what changes a culture to be more inclusive. It becomes a shared culture, not a culture of races divided, but a culture of the human race.

Most generations have their pivotal moment, that tipping point that guides the course of history for an era. Regardless of changes through the millennia, the lessons of history can always apply if for no other reason than the consistencies brought by human nature and the human condition. Human nature seems to be the one constant other than the inevitability of change. It becomes the generational charge for this new American patriot to lead change in the direction of promise and success. To continue flying the banner of American democracy at home while living in a global interdependence that is inspired by individuality, respectful of cultural diversity, erases race from the conversation and commits to equality for the human race.

NOTES

Chapter 1

Essay on *"Notes on Nationalism"* by George Orwell published in British "Magazine of Philosophy, Psychology, and Aesthetics" *Polemic*, in October 1945.

Chapter 2

Excerpt from the *Declaration of Independence*, July 1776.

Excerpt from Rights of Man by Thomas Paine, 1791.

Excerpt from Speech given by Bono at Georgetown University at an event hosted by the Global Social Enterprise Initiative and Georgetown's McDonough School of Business, Nov. 12, 2012.

The Constitution of the United States, the Bill of Rights and All Amendments

Epic of America by James Truslow Adams, 1931

Chapter 3

Leviathan by Thomas Hobbes, 1651

"*A Letter Concerning Toleration*" by John Locke, 1689

"*An Essay Concerning Human Understanding*" by John Locke, 1689

Common Sense by Thomas Paine, 1776

Excerpt from the *Declaration of Independence*, July 1776

The Constitution of the United States, the Bill of Rights and All Amendments

Chapter 4

John F. Kennedy Speech at Amherst College, October 1963

Albert Henry Woolson, Veterans Memorial Hall, Duluth, Minnesota, url: http://www.vets-hall.org/stories/civil-war/albert-woolson. (Retrieved May 2020)

WWII Veteran statistics from the Department of Veterans Affairs and the National World War II Museum url: https://www.nationalww2museum.org/war/wwii-veteran-statistics. (Retrieved May 2020)

Alexander Hamilton, *Federalist 1*, October 1787-April 1788

James Madison, *Federalist 10*. October 1787-April 1788

James Madison, *Federalist 51*. October 1787-April 1788

Chapter 5

Smith, Dwight L (1989). "A North American Neutral Indian Zone: Persistence of a British Idea". *Northwest Ohio Quarterly.*

"War of 1812". (2006). *Compton's by Britannica.* Encyclopedia Britannica Online. (Retrieved May 2020)

Ivie, Robert L. "The metaphor of force in prowar discourse: The case of 1812." *Quarterly Journal of Speech* 68#3 (1982), pp. 240-253.

Perkins, Bradford. The Causes of the War of 1812: National Honor or National Interest? (1962).

Jensen, Merrill (1959). The Articles of Confederation: An Interpretation of the Social-Constitutional History of the American Revolution, 1774–1781. University of Wisconsin Press.

https://www.theusconstitution.org/news/understanding-the-three-fifths-compromise/ (Retrieved May 2020)

https://www.history.com/topics/american-civil-war/gettysburg-address (Retrieved May 2020)

https://constitutioncenter.org (Retrieved May 2020)

Chapter 6

Adam Gopnik (August 28, 2014) "Does It Help to Know History?" *The New Yorker.*

1890 Census Bulletin (11th Census). United States Census Office. 1892. p. 2.

Clark, Cynthia L. (2011). The American Economy: A Historical Encyclopedia. ABC-CLIO. p. 397.

Walter Licht. Working for the Railroad: The Organization of Work in the Nineteenth Century (1983)

Mark Twain and Charles Dudley Warner. The Gilded Age (1873)

Bryan Burns. Lewis Ginter: Richmond's Gilded Age Icon. Charleston, SC: History Press, 2011.

"History." "The Jefferson". April 7, 2014. http://www.jeffersonhotel.com/experience/history. (Retrieved May 2020)

"Lewis Ginter." The Virginia Magazine of History and Biography 5, no. 3 (1898): 348-349.

North, David. "Major Lewis Ginter (1824-1897)." Lewis Ginter Botanical Garden. April 7, 2014. http://www.lewisginter.org/about/history/lewis_ginter_history.php.

Richmond Dispatch. Oct. 3, 1897.

Kollatz Jr., Harry (May 5, 2009), The Invisible Philanthropist; Grace Arents, a shy heiress, transformed her city, Richmond Magazine

Oregon Hill District National Park Service. https://www.nps.gov/nr/travel/richmond/OregonHillHD.html

"Grace Arents". Saint Andrew's Episcopal Church. (Retrieved May 2020)

Wade, Louise Carrol (2004). *"Settlement Houses." Encyclopedia of Chicago.* Chicago Historical Society.

National Assessment of Adult Literacy https://nces.ed.gov/naal/lit_ history.asp

Excerpts are taken from Chapter 1 of *120 Years of American Education: A Statistical Portrait* (Edited by Tom Snyder, National Center for Education Statistics, 1993).

Chernow, Ron. Grant. Penguin Random House. 2017

Chapter 7

Benson, Donald. The Moment of Proof : Mathematical Epiphanies, pp. 172–173 (Oxford University Press, 1999).

Diamond, Jared. Guns, Germs, and Steel: The Fates of Human Societies. New York: Norton (1999).

https://list.juwai.com/news/2018/10/juwai-chinese-global-property-investment-report-2018#:~:text=The%20Juwai%20Chinese%20Global%20Property,growth%20at%20US%2425.6%20billion. (Retrieved May 2020)

Chapter 8

Ruddy, Daniel (2016), Theodore the Great: Conservative Crusader, Washington D.C.: Regnery History.

Miller, Nathan (1992). Theodore Roosevelt, A Life. William Morrow & Co.

Brands, Henry William (1997), TR: The Last Romantic (full biography), New York: Basic Books.

Dalton, Kathleen (2002), Theodore Roosevelt: A Strenuous Life. Knopf.

Excerpt from Patrick Henry's speech to the Virginia Convention 1775, St. Johns Church, Richmond, Virginia.

www.history.com/topics/world-war-i/u-s-entry-into-world-war-i-1 (Retrieved May 2020.)

Swanson, Joseph; Williamson, Samuel (1972). "Estimates of national product and income for the United States economy, 1919–1941". Explorations in Economic History. 10: 53–73

Bryant, Joyce. The Great Depression and New Deal, *Yale-New Haven Teachers Institute*

Worster, Donald (1979). Dust Bowl: The Southern Plains in the 1930s. Oxford University Press. p. 49.

Graham, Otis L., Jr. An Encore for Reform: The Old Progressives and the New Deal. New York: Oxford University Press, 1967.

Leuchtenburg, William. Franklin D. Roosevelt and the New Deal, 1932-1940. New York: Harper and Row, 1963.

Pearl Harbor Statistics: www.census.gov/history/pdf/pearl-harbor-fact-sheet-1.pdf (Retrieved May 2020)

Chapter 9

Chafe, William H. The Unfinished Journey: America Since World War II

https://wps.prenhall.com/wps/media/objects/751/769950/ Documents_Library/eoa1964.htm (Retrieved May 2020)

https://www.cnn.com/2013/09/15/world/asia/tiananmen-square / index.html (Retrieved June 2020)

Chapter 10

https://data.worldbank.org (Retrieved May 2020)

https://www.pewresearch.org/fact-tank/2019/10/17/facts-about-crime-in-the-u-s/ (Retrieved May 2020)

Ingraham, Christopher. The Washington Post. "Black men sentenced to more time for committing the exact same crime as a white person, study says." Nov. 16, 2017.

https://repository.law.umich.edu/cgi/viewcontent.cgi?article=2413 &context=articles Racial Disparity in Federal Criminal Sentences. (Retrieved June 2020)

prisonpolicy.org/reports/rates (Retrieved May 2020)

prisonstudies.org/highest-to-lowest/prison-population-total (Retrieved May 2020)

National Research Council Committee on Superfund Site Assessment (2005). *Superfund and mining megasites: lessons from the Coeur D'Alene River basin*. National Academies Press.

Atomic Homefront. HBO Documentaries. Rebecca Cammisa 2017.

Price, Austin. <u>The Earth Island Journal</u>. October 30, 2019

Gibbens, Sarah. *National Geographic*. "Massive 8,000-mile 'dead zone' could be one of the gulf's largest." June 10, 2019

https://buffalonews.com/2018/08/04/a-history-of-the-love-canal-disaster-1893-to-1998/ (Retrieved May 2020)

https://stateimpact.npr.org/pennsylvania/2020/04/17/pennsylvania-raises-alarms-on-transfer-of-radioactive-three-mile-island-reactor/ (Retrieved May 2020)

Leahy, Stephen. *National Geographic*. "Exxon Valdez changed the oil industry forever—but new threats emerge". March 22, 2019

Mann v. Ford. HBO Documentaries. Maro Chermayeff and Micah Fink. 2011.

https://owlcation.com/stem/-Ten-Worst-Man-Made-Environmental-Disasters-in-American-History (Retrieved May 2020)

Meiners, Joan. *National Geographic* . "Ten years later, BP oil spill continues to harm wildlife—especially dolphins". April 17, 2020

www.covanta.com

https://www.pewresearch.org/fact-tank/2019/06/12/5-facts-about-illegal-immigration-in-the-u-s/ (Retrieved May 2020)

Fairchild, Amy; Bateman-House, Alison (April 1, 2008). "Medical Examination of Immigrants at Ellis Island". *AMA Journal of Ethics.* 10 *(4): 235–241.*

"Before Ebola, Ellis Island's terrifying medical inspections". *PBS NewsHour.* October 15, 2014. Retrieved January 19, 2019.

Chapter 11

Fischer, David Hackett. The Revolution of American Conservatism: The Federalist Party in the Era of Jeffersonian Democracy (1965) p 116

Morris, Richard B. The Forging of the Union: 1781–1789. pp 267–97

https://www.senate.gov/artandhistory/history/minute/Washingtons_Farewell_Address.htm (Retrieved May 2020)

Chapter 12

Jung, D.L. (1996), The Federal Communications Commission, the broadcast industry, and the fairness doctrine 1981–1987, New York: University Press of America, Inc.

Chapter 13

Aldridge, A. Owen (1959). Man of Reason: The Life of Thomas Paine. Lippincott

Paine, Thomas. <u>Common Sense</u>. (1776)

Paine, Thomas. <u>Rights of Man</u>. (1791)

Paine, Thomas. <u>Age of Reason</u>. (1794)

Chapter 14

https://www.brandwatch.com/blog/history-of-facebook/ Joshua Boyd (Retrieved May 2020)

https://www.insidehighered.com/digital-learning/article/2018/11/07/new-data-online-enrollments-grow-and-share-overall-enrollment (Retrieved May 2020)

https://www.digitalcommerce360.com/article/e-commerce-sales-retail-sales-ten-year-review/ (Retrieved May 2020)

https://www.pewresearch.org/internet/2018/12/10/artificial-intelligence-and-the-future-of-humans/ (Retrieved May 2020)

Chapter 15

Johns Hopkins Corona Virus Resource Center https://coronavirus.jhu.edu/

Romero, Anna Maria. *The Independent.* "Like it or Not, Asians have been Wearing Masks for over a Century…" March 6, 2020

https://www.pewresearch.org/fact-tank/2020/06/03/10-things-we-know-about-race-and-policing-in-the-u-s/ (Retrieved June 2020)

https://www.ted.com/talks/dr_phillip_atiba_goff_rashad_robinson_
dr_bernice_king_anthony_d_romero_the_path_to_ending_
systemic_racism_in_the_us/transcript (Retrieved June 2020)

https://www.vox.com/2014/6/3/5775918/25-years-after-tiananmen-
most-chinese-univeristy-students-have-never (Retrieved June 2020)

Chapter 16

https://www.statista.com/statistics/797321/us-population-
by-generation

ACKNOWLEDGMENTS

The [*New*] New Patriotism was not the original path I imagined as a new author. As I followed America's journey through its remarkable history, it resurrected forgotten gratitude I feel as an American. We live in a country of extraordinary beauty that attracted Founders of equally impressive vision to create an enduring foundation for this country. The American Founders deserve a major shout out of praise and gratitude. We would not live this version of American life we do, without them.

I have tremendous respect, love, and thanks to give to my husband Jeff, who has a big life already with his career, devotion to our family of six children, and me. Jeff was always available when asked to read chapters, drafts, and rewrites. He provided valuable feedback and patience as I recounted data and statistics.

I am so grateful to my Mom and Dad. They provided insightful feedback and perspective from a generation that has lived more history than I. A deep appreciation goes to my Dad for creating a learning environment steeped in history and literature, encouraging curiosity and thought.

Major thanks to my readers: Tyler and Catie Frech, Renu Brennan, Jane Goddard, Dana Konovalov, and Maury Anderson. I can't tell you how much I appreciate the time and attention you gave to this book around your busy lives.